The

Heart of Sales

Practical Sales Skills
for People Who Choose to Trade Ethically

Jane Binnion

JANE BINNION BOOKS

Published in the United Kingdom by **Jane Binnion Books**

www.janebinnion.com
@janebinnion

Designed by **The Dog Ate My Bookshop**
Printed version typeset in Optima on Crown Royal
Design ©2015 The Dog Ate My Bookshop

Electronic version ©2015
Copyright ©2015
ISBN 978-0-9934586-0-6

To my daughter Isabella
who inspires almost all I do.

To those who choose
to live their life awake.

Reviews of Kindle Edition

Sales is still a fairly taboo topic. As a result, a book on the 'heart of sales' might seem self-contradictory – after all, it's drummed into us that sales is by its very nature totally heartless.

The Heart of Sales, a how-to guide for start-ups and small businesses that choose to trade ethically, leads the reader step-by-step though the pre-sale, sale, and post-sale processes. Although the book is about on ethical sales, the 'ethics bit' is integrated subtly into the prose, proving from the start that it can be incorporated easily into practice. The main focus of *The Heart of Sales* seems to be 'it's all about relationships', making it at times read like a dating guide – minus the cheesy chat-up lines.

Jane writes without flaunting any esoteric jargon, making the book readable and accessible to readers with any level of business experience. The upbeat tone of Jane's writing might not be to everyone's taste; for example, being told to 'give yourself a big pat on the back' won't go down well in some circles. Nonetheless, it must be noted that Jane's sincerity is unquestionable: her genuineness and openness throughout the book show that these encouragements are definitely intended to reassure, the book leaves the reader feeling motivated - and more importantly, empowered - about the daunting prospect of starting a business.

The Heart of Sales is a recommended read for people starting in sales or wishing to brush up their sales skills – or indeed, anyone who wants an up-to-date and clear-cut analysis of sales in the present day. With her expertise and insight, Jane has transformed the traditional competitive nature of sales and provided a model that is altogether more human; this book is undeniably written from the heart.

Hannah Snashall
Project Coordinator, Lancaster District Chamber of Commerce

"As a solopreneur I found this book so useful. I've certainly found the sales process challenging at times in the 6 years I've been running my own business and I love the way Jane breaks it down into manageable, clear steps.

Many of the women business owners I work with feel 'icky' when it comes to sales because of negative past experiences and I would certainly recommend this book to them, as Jane totally reframes the idea of sales.

I found this so easy to read and know it's a book I'll refer to time and time again.

Whether you're a one-man-band or a larger business, I highly recommend *The Heart of Sales*."

Nicola Humber
Hypnotherapist and Abundance Coach

"As a digital app publisher, I get to read many articles and found Jane's new book *The Heart of Sales* to be well written, informative and easy to read.

With inspiring quotes from many heart-centered people of the last 100-years, this book will help you to gain a better insight into the way we should all market our businesses authentically and keep true to ourselves. I particularly loved the content layout, which built out on and included regular tasks and goals, to encourage the reader to reflect on their current business practice and to help them to develop new strategies for ethical selling."

Emma Burford
Founder & Publisher www.BusinessRocks.co

Contents

A Word from a Sponsor

By Mark Keating

*"Those who do not learn from history
are doomed to repeat it..."[1]*

This should be a first time, if not unique, experience. Yet for the second time in recent history I find myself writing the sponsorship text for a book that Shadowcat Systems (http://www.shadow.cat) supported via crowdsourcing.

The first time that I performed this task was to back a book called The Empty House (http://bit.ly/theemptyhouse) from MXPublishing (http://bit.ly/mxpublishing). The Empty House named for a Sherlock Holmes story was a book of short stories and poems by famous people who are also Holmes fans. The book was created to raise money for the Undershaw Preservation Trust which seeks to purchase the home of Sir Arthur Conan Doyle and preserve it for the public. MXPublishing used crowdsourcing to raise money to have the book translated into three more languages to increase its sales and raise more funds. Matt and I have always been Holmes fans,[2] and so it was a no brainer for us to sponsor this effort.

What transpired during the crowdsourced process was moderately unusual for both us and the publishers. There were only supposed to be three new language versions, with a 'larger' sponsor for each We chose to back the Spanish Language version. However, the fund raised enough money to translate the book into six languages, not the intended three, and Shadowcat became the largest individual sponsor with most people opting for just a reward (book of their choice) not to just back the project. As a reward for our generosity we were given a page in each copy, translated into the respective

---

1 George Santayana. Sometimes happily so.

2 I often see myself as the affable Doctor to Matt's Holmes is we played out those roles.

language, to talk about Shadowcat and our decision to sponsor the book and became the language translation sponsors.

So although this is not the first time I have written a sponsor text it does represent a first. This is the first time I have written this text and will be able to read it in the published book in English.

So you repeated...[3]

There are an inevitable couple of questions that I should answer for you now. Why did we decide to back another book from crowdsourcing? Why this book?

Crowdsourcing is Liberty

My background is a Literature graduate who then worked in publishing for a decade before starting Shadowcat Systems with Matt. The publishing company I worked for, Carnegie Publishing (http://bit.ly/carnegiepublishing), produced local history books, but they also helped other small publishers and self-publishers to get their book published.

This has always left a love of writers and the publishing process in me.[4] There is also a great fondness for the small publisher, local publisher and self-publisher as many of the people I encountered in my former career matched those criteria.

The advent of crowdfunding of books is often touted as a modern approach and as a divergent or revolution in publishing. I do not believe that. Before the advent of large publishing houses and mass consumption of books, a fascination that started its most prominent period at the latter part of the nineteenth century and dominated the twentieth, many books were privately published. In fact much of what we see as crowdfunding matches the great publishing patrons

---

3 If I sponsor a third book in this manner then I have to ask one of the SC programmers to script it and release the module as Open Source, it's just a thing we do.

4 It has also left scars and a great deal of anecdotes.

of the nineteenth century who would sponsor the publication of works and more importantly libraries.

The patronage of libraries, mostly traveling libraries, resulted in an enormous shift of the landscape in writing and reading. For the first time large numbers of women, and those of lower incomes, had access to literature and they consumed it voraciously. This led to libraries sponsoring the publication of books written by women (http://bit.ly/circlibraries), in particular the novel.

In this regard we can see that crowdfunding, patronage, and small-scale self-publication was a contributory factor in the release from emancipation. If we sponsor someone's efforts we are in fact empowering them by removing the restrictions placed on them: by political infrastructure in regards to financial status and ability; society, in particular by social stereotype and access; by popularity, the publishing predilection for big name authors. The access to novels and factual books complemented the education of a generation and changed how they perceived themselves and their place in the world. Open access via sponsorship, based on merit not name, is liberty.

Why Jane?

I first met Jane a few years ago at a meeting of ethical traders in Lancaster. Our early relationship was probably quite cautious, I am a fairly outspoken person[5] and can seem dominating with my large frame and loud voice. Jane is a polite, intelligent and friendly person who thankfully can also hold her own weight in a conversation so isn't easily cowed.[6]

---

5 That's putting it very mildly. I am a confident speaker and I read a lot and say a lot. I have never claimed to have all the facts but I can have a rough stab at something approaching them.

6 One of my largest concerns is that I am often seen as dominating due to my height, loud voice and ability to talk the legs of a donkey. It concerns me that this might intimidate people which I have no desire to do as I love talking to people and learning about them.

I would love to say that we became firm friends from the outset, but this isn't an Enid Blyton world. We did have a great deal of mutual respect as we both read similar articles and followed trends. It was, however, on the matter of equality that I think we found a basis for strong friendship. Jane is an ardent supporter of the need for equality in the world, and is to many outspoken in her views regarding the need to re-evaluate and equalise the genders, removing bias.

I personally do not see Jane as outspoken, I would be happy if she said more. I think the use of the word outspoken is often a subconscious, and sometimes conscious, desire to negate a rational argument with negative description. I have a strong wish to see an equal footing for every person regardless of gender, ethnicity, viewpoints, education or fiscal status. It was this that gave Jane and I a mutual respect that we have built upon. We are comfortable being treated as equals by each other; personally I feel honoured by this.

For this reason I have always been proud to support Jane's efforts and her various projects. But that is on a personal status, how about Shadowcat Systems?

Shadowcat are what I like to call 'good community players'. We are an Open Source Consultancy, we are members of the Free/Libre Open Source Software Organisation, the Perl Foundation, Enlightened Perl Organisation, Lancaster and Morecambe Makers (http://lamm.hackspace.org.uk),[7] Lancaster Social to name a few. We regularly release free code and support projects, run conferences and events and play a part in local and global business and professional communities. Part of our ethical structure is of collaboration, encouragement and support. It was a no-brainer to the Shadowcat team to support and sponsor one of Jane's earlier initiatives that was Lancashire's first Women's Conference.

When Jane first announced she was crowdsourcing her book I had no hesitation in helping, however much I could, to spread the word. But I also knew that Shadowcat would sponsor. I left our sponsorship

---

7 Lancaster and Morecambe Makers: Mailing List is: http://bit.ly/lammlist - Facebook Group can be found at: http://bit.ly/lammface - IRC channel: #lamm on irc.freenode.org - Github Repository is: http://bit.ly/lammgit - Email address is: LAMMspace@gmail.com

until the eleventh hour on purpose, I knew we would put money towards it, but I wanted to ensure it was enough to make the book a success. This book deserved to be written.

Jane carries a strong ethical stance, moral authority and decency. She is a single mother and businesswoman who has had to carve out a place in an often male-dominated industry. To raise a child well is hard, to do so on your own is easily doubly hard. To run a successful business is hard, to do so with as a lone parent is a massive challenge. But, to do both while sticking to strong ethical principles and supporting a range of community initiatives is the mark of someone special.

Jane is a strong example of how we can all do better and how we can stand by our beliefs and do well without compromising our principles. When she wanted to write a book talking about how to do this in business it was a privilege as a company based on community and the empowerment of individuals and organisations to support her.

Mark Keating
June 2015

Foreword

By Phil M Jones

As infants most of us had the ability to get more of what we wanted purely by asking for it. Parents soon taught us that it is rude to ask and that myth has since lived on in many adults across the globe. Unfortunately there are very few people growing up today and longing to work in sales. In fact the very thought of being a 'sales person" has many people cringing at the pure thought of it.

I have spent the bulk of my professional career helping my customers to buy before continuing with my mission to "teach the world to sell" and change the belief that selling is not a dirty word. Done right the art of selling is a service, a gift and a real pleasure for everybody involved. The reality is that everybody is selling something and the success of many small businesses relies on its ability to help others see the value in their offerings.

Starting in business can be daunting and failing to generate sufficient revenue can stop many businesses before they get started. Learning to sell in a professional way that delivers value to all parties can go a long way to assisting that success and resulting in your business dream continuing to reality that fulfills the promises you make to your customers.

Today's digital age leads to a level of transparency that levels the playing fields and means that every business, regardless of size, is now vulnerable to its reputation. What selling certainly does not mean is to over embellish, fabricate the truth or promise anything more than you truly believe is possible. In my eyes selling is simply earning the right to make a recommendation.

Working with Jane since 2012 I have continually been impressed with her tenacity, professionalism and ability to serve her local business community. When it comes to **Ethical Sales**, Jane really is a product of her own words and has crafted these lessons from an abundance of collected and well-practiced experience.

Selling ethically is really the only way it should be done. There are no short cuts, no dirty tricks and no foul play. Reading this book clearly demonstrates what it takes to stand out from your competition for the right reasons, assist them through the buying process and have them keep coming back for more.

Whether you have just started in business or are looking for some simple guidance this simple guide delivers you a systematic approach to sales married with a set of values perfect for today's business world.

Phil M Jones
www.philmjones.com

Preface

With a degree in sociology and 20 years working as a Youth and Community worker, I'm a very unlikely entrepreneur. And yet here I am, running my own business and loving it! I've had to face the same challenges as everyone else and find myself here in 2015, having survived a terrible recession and totally excited about what's coming next.

I took the leap into running my training business full time in 2011. I trained in social media and then, because I saw organisation after organisation struggling due to the lack of a strategy, I trained in business education with international sales speaker and trainer, Phil M. Jones.

I found that I wasn't comfortable with the traditional sales training, so I started designing and testing material based on ethical trading and in 2013 I launched the Naked Sales Trainer, bringing ethical sales skills to town.

I decided to write this book after meeting so many wonderful people with brilliant services and products, but who just were not comfortable with the 'whole sales thing' and therefore were not growing their businesses in the way that they wanted. Knowing that so many small business owners struggle with selling I wanted to pull my experiences and training materials together to create a simple guide to selling ethically.

The Big Picture

The United Kingdom is becoming the 'self-employment capital' of Western Europe.[8] From the beginning of 2013 to 2014 there were 197,000 new sole trader businesses in the UK.[9] We are seeing a wave of individuals wanting to make a difference setting up business

8 http://bit.ly/JBUKEmployment
9 http://bit.ly/JBSoleTraders

as sole traders and social enterprises are being launched at a rapid rate of knots.

A nation with that structure clearly needs to know how to sell its products and services if there is going to be economic growth.

In the UK approximately 50% of all businesses fail in the first two years.[10] It breaks my heart to see small business owner after small business owner work their butts off only to fail because they do not know how to sell.

So this book is for all of us who want to grow a sustainable, profitable, business without compromising our values.

This book is by no means brought to you as the definitive guide to sales - I learn something new every week. What it is, is a pulling together of my mistakes, my learning, my research and my observations.

Bringing all that together to produce a simple, easy to read, self-training book on ethical sales skills has been no small challenge and I am hugely grateful to the many people who have given me support and encouragement, their time, and good thinking.

I have written this book as a trainer and at the end of each section there are prompts to record your action points. I encourage you to write down what you are going to implement with a 'done by date' because we are more likely to act on things that we commit to paper. Do take the time to revisit these action points to review and reflect.

Plans change and need to be flexible. If you have met your targets then celebrate because one thing is for sure, running a business is not the easy option, it's plain hard work. Rewarding our achievements is essential.

---

10 http://bit.ly/JBsmallbusiness

I never said it
would be easy,
***I only said it would
be worth it***
- Mae West

Introduction

The Rules Have Changed

We are in an age where collaboration, not competition, gets the big win. An age where connection is becoming all-important and transparency and accountability are demanded. A time when people have a voice and are using it, a time when people are choosing to trade with people they Know, Like and Trust. And I am excited! Because for all of us who started our business, social enterprise, or charity to make a difference, this is our time. Business influencers from Richard Branson, Rachel Elnaugh and Guy Kawasaki are all talking about the need to set up businesses that make the world a better place.

If we run a business we need to be able to sell. But there is a mystique around sales and many contradictions. We need to sell, but being called a 'Good Salesman' is not a compliment.

I read a while ago that business schools don't teach sales because it's the 'dirty side' of business. Actually sales is the heart of a business. Without sales we don't have a business and sales should absolutely not be dirty.

People need to buy things and we need to sell them. By getting organised, being customer focused and going through the right steps at the right time, you may well discover that you come to love sales because, after all, how great is it to help someone to find the very thing they need. And let's face it you wouldn't have set up your particular organisation if you didn't think there was a need, would you?

This is now a time when we can transform the sales process into a win:win. Selling great products and services to people who want and need them - without compromising our value base.

If you love your product or service and you want to make a difference then this book is for you.

This book is a Bullshit-free training guide to selling without compromising your values. The aim of this book is to de-mystify the sales process and provide you with a framework to use to increase your connections, gain more paying customers AND keep them. In other words, this book is about building a sustainable, solid, ethical business.

This is not a Blue Peter, here's one I made earlier, do it just like this book. This book shares ideas and tips for you to adapt for your own business, enabling you to take some space and do good thinking. Some of the best advice I've ever heard is have an open mind and think, "oh that's interesting, I wonder how I can apply that to my business".

In the appendices you will find two Q&As, one from a charity and one from a start-up, that you may find useful as they answer the main questions that get raised in sales.

And the great news is... just by reading this book you are already ahead of the game as most business owners do not take the time to study, review, reflect and learn.

So go you! ☺

Section 1: The Heart of Sales?

What is Ethical Sales All About?

Many people associate ethical sales with the Fairtrade movement. Of course the Fairtrade movement is a very successful example of trading that ensures some of the most exploited people are paid a fair price for their labour and products. But that is only one aspect. We can all choose to sell ethically and there are a whole heap of reasons why that's a good plan.

Essentially, trading ethically is all about integrity and that is where people think sales is at odds with their value base, as the commonly held belief is that integrity and sales are not two words that easily go together.

So in this section we will look at:

* What is ethical selling?

* A brief history of ethical trade.

* The relevance for businesses today.

In a Nutshell

Ethical sales is about:

* Selling a good product for a fair price

* Valuing and respecting your customers, your suppliers and your staff team

* Not trying to trick people into buying things they don't need or want just to make a sale

* Transparency - being truthful as to what your product or service provides

21

* Social connectivity - understanding the bigger picture of community and the planet

* Collaboration above competition

* Avoiding waste of resources

An ethical trader is not someone who is out to make a quick buck at the expense of the planet and its inhabitants.

If most of the above ring true for you, then you are probably very interested in trading ethically.

> *If you want to make money get a job, running a business is about making a difference*
>
> Wayne Hemmingway

My experience is that most people who set up a small business, or not-for-profit organisation, do so to make a difference.

However, ethical selling does not mean that you cannot, or should not, make a profit. In fact, the reverse is true. If you don't make a profit you are not running a sustainable organisation. Of course, very few of us make a profit in the first couple of years; however, if we maintain a negative income we will simply have to cease trading.

A Brief History of Ethical Sales

Some of the companies that trade with an ethical head on and are making a good profit are: Green and Blacks, Brompton Bikes and Ecover, but selling ethically is not a new concept.

It was a decision to sell ethically back in 1824 that grew the Quaker businesses Cadbury and Rowntree. At a time when bartering was the norm, Cadbury chose to set a fair price for their chocolate and people liked that they knew what they were getting for their money.

"They had a reputation for honesty and reliability, along with a quest for justice, equality and social reform." People knew that these companies treated their staff exceptionally well for a Victorian

England that was still using child labour. It was their ethical stance that created such loyalty amongst consumers that meant Cadbury, Fry's and Rowntree virtually monopolised the confectionery market for over 100 years.[11]

Rowntree, Fry's and Cadbury are just some of a number of successful Quaker businesses that were faith led. In doing my research for this book I found that most, if not all, religious texts offer guidance regarding the importance of trading fairly and not being motivated by greed. Thus the call to trade ethically is as old as religion itself.

How is Ethical Trade Relevant Today?

We appear to be in a new age of transparency and accountability. People want to know more about the companies with whom they are dealing and they are willing to search for that information using the power afforded by the Internet. Bad, or poor, behaviour, in all sectors, is being exposed on a daily basis and then shared and commented upon. I'm an ethical trader because I couldn't be anything else. However, in the modern age it just makes good economic sense.

Let's start with some facts that may surprise you:

During our recent recession there were 2 markets that didn't just survive, but thrived.

1. The luxury goods market - At this end of the market there seems to be no such thing as a recession. For example: the merged French luxury goods provider of Louis Vuitton and Moët Hennessy saw its combined sales jump from €17.2bn in 2008 to over €30bn in 2013.[12]

2. Ethical goods and services – A shift in culture is resulting in the UK population increasingly choosing to spend their limited money on products that give value, not cause damage.

---

11 BBC Jan 2010 (http://news.bbc.co.uk/1/hi/magazine/8467833.stm)

12 http://cfi.co/lifestyle/2014/05/luxury-goods-market-crisis-what-crisis/

A quarter of UK consumers said they would buy Fairtrade products, organic foods and green cleaning products even if it cost them more money.

Guardian Aug 2013 [13]

The annual Ethical Consumer Markets Report of 2012 showed that since the onset of the recession:

> *The total value of ethical markets has gone from £35.5bn to £47.2bn. Amongst the biggest growing categories during the recession are:*
>
> *Sustainable fish up 323% from £69m to £292m. Fairtrade products which have increased 176 % from £458m to £1,262m and free-range eggs sales up 78% cent from £444m to £792m"* [14]

Change is coming and it's coming fast!

In 1934 Edward A. Filene wrote:

> *It takes a good businessman to provide good service. If he doesn't give good service, he knows his customers will not come back, while the goods he has sold them will.* [15]

Since Filene's time there has been considerable change in business practice. In the 1980s we saw a rise in individualism and a break down in community. Customer care pretty much fell off the agenda and making a profit seemed to become the be all and end all. Without a doubt, things got out of balance and this has had a long lasting impact. But that was not sustainable and as a result things are changing again.

The rise of social media over the last decade means that more people than ever now have a voice - and they are using it. Unethical behaviour is being exposed on a daily basis. Organisations that

---

13 http://bit.ly/JBEthicalshopping

14 http://bit.ly/ethicalconsumer2012

15 Morals in Business1934 Edward A. Filene:
http://labs.theguardian.com/unicef-child-labour/

thought they were exempt from accountability are learning that change is coming and it's coming fast.

Consumers have gotten tired of the lack of accountability and are expecting better service again. People are talking across the globe and transparency and accountability are the new rules. News travels so fast that, if nothing else, people are changing their behaviour out of embarrassment.

Filene's statement is again true. It is just not sustainable, in this new business era, to trade unethically.

With our new communication channels, the ability to hide is increasingly difficult, as a result there is a growing trend towards **radical transparency**. The Co-Op report [16] found that 33% of consumers want to know the backstory of an organisation. So whilst governments drag their feet over ecological issues, forward thinking businesses are just getting on with it. For example, Ecover are funding research into using algae as an alternative to palm oil[17] and Chipotle are growing a massive loyalty as they openly promote their commitment to supporting improved animal welfare policy and practice.[18]

Our demand for transparency has resulted in companies who share information about themselves and make a public commitment to change. These organisations are not only ahead of the game in customer relations but they increase their profit margin. Being sustainable is not only saving money, it significantly increases loyalty and in return sales.

If this section has inspired you to implement something new, or do more of something you already do, then take some time now to write down the items in the following table.

---

16 Additional Resource. *Child Labour in the Fashion Supply Chain*
http://bit.ly/ethicalconsumer2012

17 http://bit.ly/guardianpalmoil

18 http://wellmoney.net/chipotle-sacrifices-short-term-sales-for-long-term-principles

Task One	
Action Points	
Done by Date	
Review Date	

Section 2: Preparing You

Preparing

In sales, as in all aspects of life, we will be more successful if we prepare well. And the most important, yet most overlooked bit of preparation that needs doing is with our self.

The aim of this section is to take time to look at our self, because we take all of ourselves into business with us. Whether you are a sole trader, or head up a 100-person staff team, the bottom line is that people run businesses.

If things go right, it's down to us and if things go wrong, that's also down to us. So understanding ourselves and how we sometimes get in our own way, or even self-sabotage, is the most important first step. This is also an area that is usually neglected in traditional sales training.

We will look at why we set up our organisation, our self-sabotage patterns, our weaknesses and strengths, our feelings about money and preparing ourselves for selling.

One

Preparing Yourself

There is currently a movement that says that if you develop a heart based business; everything else will just fall into place. Guy Kawasaki wrote: "If you make meaning you'll probably make money".[19] I am clear that it is important to be in a business that you love and that when you do something from a place of love there is a different energy. Certainly if we don't (mostly) love our business then we probably should not be doing it, because running a business is not a 9 to 5 job, we pretty much live and breathe it. But, loving what you do in itself is not enough, there are a number of essential elements required to create and build a sustainable organisation. We are going to start to address these here.

What is success?

One issue that creates disillusionment for so many business owners is the myth that some people just have what it takes to become an overnight success, which means that those who have worked hard and are not now millionaires have failed.

One of the biggest mistakes we can make is to compare ourselves to others and find ourselves lacking, because we are rarely comparing like with like. So taking time to fully know what success means to you is possibly the most important first step to building our confidence and focus.

Success is traditionally defined as bigger, faster, flashier and more expensive, but we are now in an age where we are rethinking that.

---

19 Guy Kawasaki - The Art of the start 2

What is your definition of success?

It's all too easy to get bogged down in the stress of the day-to-day of it all and forget why we are actually doing what we do.

As a single mum, I set up my business to allow me to work from home so that I could give my daughter the time she needed and look after my own health.

I've done a great job of both of those and I'm building a thriving business. Sometimes I have to remind myself not to buy into someone else's definition of success, because the truth is that our lives are different and I love my life. I have learned to check myself when I see men I know jetting off around the world and I think that this means they are doing so much better than me.

Some people might not think that raising a healthy, well-adjusted child who has had some pretty cool adventures is a success. I am totally sure it is. The fact that I have been a role model for her and shown her that we can do it differently, on our terms, is an added bonus.

My definition of success

* Time to be there for, and hang out with, my wonderful daughter;

* Make enough money to travel and have adventures;

* Time to write;

* Self-determination;

* Good health.

I am not rich,
I don't have an expensive car,
but I am very happy.

Success is liking yourself, *liking what you do,* and liking how *you do it.*
- Maya Angelou

Task Two

So this task is to take 10 minutes to remind yourself:

* Why you set up (or are setting up) your organisation
* What do you value in life?

My definition of success is...

What's important in my life is...

Now write those down and put them on display somewhere where you will see them every day to remind yourself of your purpose

Identifying your self-sabotage patterns

Now that you have reminded yourself what you are working towards, let's look at whether you are **getting in your own way**. Getting our head in the right place is essential in most activities and it certainly is in selling. There is clear evidence that people, who are not able to grow their business in the manner that they want, are often holding themselves back by their lack of self-belief and doubts such as:

* Can I do this?

* Will people actually pay for this?

* Am I good enough?

We sabotage in many ways and you can probably add a few of your own negative self talk messages. I worked with someone who really wanted to sell their art but they were unable to diary time to paint. We worked out that his messages was 'painting isn't real work'.

"Success is on the other side of your comfort zone."

Orrin Woodward

Many of us were taught to not promote ourselves. Certainly my life in the public sector meant that I made all sorts of good stuff happen but promoted the brand, not myself. I hid behind the larger organisation at all times. As a result, I needed to seriously shift out of my comfort zone when it came to going out there promoting myself (my business). You know that you are moving out of your comfort zone when it feels as scary as heck!

Seth Godin[20] talks about the *lizard brain*, which was the voice in the back of his head when he was starting out in business. The lizard brain is only interested in finding food, reproducing and surviving. It needs us to stay put because stepping outside our safe zone means there may be lions, or something equally scary, waiting to eat us!

Running a business exposes us and will bring up a whole heap of insecurities.

During a big business wobble, a friend said to me **'we take ourselves into our business'**, meaning that any insecurities we had before we started our business were not left at the door of our new office; they came right in and plonked themselves on our shoulder to have a little word in our ear whenever things got a little risky.

Our ability to keep moving forward and take risks depends on our ability to face our demons, insecurities and fears head on. We will wobble, and the scarier it feels the more we will wobble.[21] Sadly, in business culture wobbles are not often discussed. Have you been to networking events where everyone feels that they have to pretend that everything is totally awesome and business has never been better? It obviously isn't always true, but whilst we perpetuate the myth, it serves to reinforce that we are not good enough.

---

20 http://vimeo.com/5895898

21 I set up The Wobble Club on Facebook for this reason. If you want a safe space to wobble then you are welcome to join: http://bit.ly/jbwobble

Whilst writing this book I had dealings with two companies who I've known for a while and who sell similar things. What I really noticed this time is that when presented with an opportunity, Company One follows up immediately and just goes for it, whilst Company 2 has a tendency to put a negative spin on things and essentially:

a) Talk themselves out of the opportunity before they even know the facts.

b) Deter people from making future referrals, as the response is so negative.

For Company 2, business has always been a struggle and I realised that is now their mindset. Their first response to new business opportunities is that it will be another struggle. The result is that Company One grows and Company Two is having to downsize.

Do you want safe or do you want to grow your business?

Personally I'm someone who gets excited about new opportunities. I have plenty of blocks, of course, and I am perfectly capable of self-sabotage - writing this book certainly brought my lizard brain to the fore! But I also recognise my ability to get excited, listen and lean into *let's give it a go.*

I don't expect every idea to work, but without exploring ideas we will never know. And now when an idea scares me, I decide that is what I need to do!

Task Three

How do you respond to new business opportunities?

Do you think that you ever self-sabotage because you don't believe that you can be, or should be, successful?

How do you self sabotage?

Jot your thoughts down so that you can see in writing
what your blocks may be.

Two

Let's Talk About Money!

As ethical traders, it's possible that we have some negative feelings when it comes to money, after all **money is the root of all evil** right? Or is it?

If we have blocks about making money, we are more likely to sabotage our sales when we see good contracts coming our way. So that is what we're going to look at next.

Task Four
Without giving it too much thought, write down the words that come to mind when you think about MONEY.
Now take a look at those words, what do they tell you about your relationship with money?

I was raised in a hard-working family where there was always more week than money. As a result, I have some values that I really like, for example, I reject the throwaway culture and I have raised my daughter to save up for the things she wants. However, I am also aware that I have a mindset of *we have enough we will manage*. It never occurred to me that we should have *more than enough*.

I had no image of myself as thriving financially. But then I thought back to my days of two full-time incomes, no kids and a tiny mortgage. A time when I actually had **spare** money. I had money that I didn't know what to do with!

Did it make me evil? Nope. Did it make me unhappy? Nope, life was good. I still worked hard, I still lived simply, I travelled because that's what I love doing, and I gave money away to people who needed it more than me.

Task Five
Thinking back to your values. What would you do if you had money in abundance? Write down what you would spend it on

When we create an image of us having a positive relationship with money, we are much more willing to let money into our lives and less likely to sabotage the contracts that pay handsomely.[22][23]

---

22 I worked with a very smart woman, Nicola Humber, on this issue and If you would like to explore money issues further she is happy to offer you a free 30 minute session. To book a call with her just visit:
http://nicolahumber.com/compcoachingcallheartofsales/

23 If you would like to read more on this go to
http://www.janebinnion.com/thoughts-ethics-making-money/

Money and Success don't change people

they merely Amplify *what is already there*

- Will Smith

Before we move onto preparing ourselves for the task of selling this is a really good time to take 10 minutes to list your business strengths.

Task Six
Write down:
All your skills, all the things that you know you are good at.
All the things that you love about running your business.

It's so easy to forget what it is that we are good at, especially during challenging times. But our strengths are what will make us feel confident in dealings with others and selling our wonderful products.

Preparing Ourselves for Selling

So many people I talk to say "I hate selling". There are a number of reasons for this which we will explore throughout the book. The most common one comes from negative experiences of being **sold to**.

We have a dilemma...

We have to sell our products and services, but not many people want to be sold to. So what can we do?

Any sales trainer will tell you that buying is an emotional experience, and yet business owners and sales staff forget that time after time. I don't know about you, but a negative experience, a grumpy sales person, or to be honest, an unreasonably long queue, will put me right off buying, because that all tells me that the owner has forgotten the importance of the customer experience. They took their eye off the ball.

Sadly, like far too many people, I've had lots of bad experiences: they would fill a book all by themselves. One experience, when I was trying to pay my credit card bill whilst grieving the death of a dear friend, shocked me so much it inspired one of my first business blogs, "Training human sales staff."[24]

The company saw the blog and sent me a nice bunch of flowers, but the experience was so awful that, three years later, I still can't set foot in that bank.

On the other hand, I have had many good experiences with traders who I now trust, such as our local mechanic. David France started out as a 2-man garage at a time when mechanics specialised in confusing and terrifying the rest of us! He has grown his business significantly because he treats his customers really well. He knows us, is generous and talks to us as one human to another. We now Know, Like and Trust him and I wouldn't dream of going anywhere else.

---

24 http://www.janebinnion.com/training-human-sales-staff

I can see that it is perhaps easier for micro businesses to build good relationships, but a positive experience in a larger store also created loyalty in me.

A few years ago I went into a shop looking for an item for my daughter. This was in the days when a sales representative was available to help you, so I asked if they had the particular item. The woman told me that they didn't, but then went on to tell me where I could find it. Now I don't know what her boss would have said, would she have been expected to sell me an alternative version of what I wanted? That shop didn't get that sale, but because they were so helpful they became my first point of call from then on.

This reinforced for me that when our intention is to help someone we, more often than not, create a strong and lasting relationship.

Most people would agree that when we have a good experience with a trader, we use them again and we tell people, because we all want more good experiences and fewer negative ones.

Thinking about your experiences, what decisions have you made in terms of how you would like to treat your customers?

I want sales staff to give me all the information I need to make a decision. That is actually pretty hard to get nowadays, so I make sure that I do that for my potential customers. If I can't help them, I make a point of referring them to someone who can, and lo and behold, most come back to me at a later date.

Task Seven

Firstly I'd like you to take a few minutes to think back to a time when you had a negative experience as a customer. Think about the scenario, what happened and how you felt. Now write down:

1. What was the experience?

2. How did it leave you feeling?

3. What decisions did you make as a result of that experience?

Now think about a time when you enjoyed buying something.

1. What was the experience?

2. What exactly was it that made it enjoyable?

3. What decisions did you make as a result of that experience?

If you have decided to take some action, make a note of the action points with done by dates and dates for reviewing them.

Three

Finance and Goal Setting

Many of us have set up a business because we have a great product to sell, a passion, or have a need to be creative. We are good at what we do but often the skills needed to run a business are not our strengths. We are creative and that other stuff seems tedious and boring! And this is where we can fall on our bums. Getting ourselves organised with our finances and our goal setting means creating a solid foundation from which we will grow.

Finance

If we think back to self-sabotage and our relationship with money in the previous chapter, it's easy to understand that a big reason for small organisations failing is that they do not put in the time to do the sums. Knowing how much you **need** to make and **want** to make, is crucial and that is what we will be covering here. It doesn't have to be complicated: initially just a simple good housekeeping type system will be a big help because, without this information, we cannot make plans, and without plans we are just drifting.

For various reasons many, many people do not keep an eye on the book-keeping, identify the areas of waste, or even have any idea actually how much is coming in and going out each month.

What has this got to do with sales training?

The bottom line is that without this information we do not know how much money we need to bring in and without that information we will not be focused on our sales needs.

Some simple sums will tell you:

What is the minimum you need to bring in over the next six to twelve months to pay your essentials such as your suppliers, your insurance, networking membership, rent, replace stock?

For example:

1. I needed a new computer. I can't work without one and so this became a priority expense. I had to find out how much it would cost so that I could work out how much extra I needed to bring in to pay for it without leaving myself with a cash flow problem.

2. This summer we want to have three weeks on Vancouver Island.

I need to work out:

* How much the holiday costs me in terms of travel and accommodation.
* How much I need for spending while we are there.
* How much it will cost me to leave my business for 3 weeks.
* If I need £10,000 to cover all that, I then am able to work out:
    ** How many additional contracts do I need and
    ** How much each contract will be worth.

For example that would require 20 contracts at £500 each.

When I take time to plan my outgoings in that way I can be much more focused on my income needs.

Next: in terms of growth targets, what would that look like?

If you want to grow your business by 20% each year for the next four years, how will you actually do that?

* What does that look like in £s and
* What does it mean in terms of new contracts?

The questions you need to keep asking yourself in each planning season is:

* How many new customers do I need?
* How much will they pay?
* And what do I need to do to make that happen?

We have become a credit economy and have paid a big price for that. Increasingly good business advice is to grow your business organically, not rely on business loans. By seeing your business this way, you are in control and you will see if your plans are realistic.

As a single mum, and with my family background, I am good at managing money and seeing things in terms of *that contract will pay for that*. But I realise many people are a bit frightened of the money management side of things, so if this is a difficult area for you, ask your accountant to help you with your financial planning. A good accountant will be delighted to see that as part of their role. After all, if your business fails then they lose a customer.

Ostrich position, fingers crossed and wishing are all common approaches to finance, but they do not make for an effective business strategy!

Task Eight
List your predicted outgoings for the next 6 months.
How much do you need to make just to cover those?
How many sales do you need to make at what unit cost, to bring that amount in?
How much do you want to make on top of that?
How many sales do you need to make at what unit cost, to make that happen?

Some Thoughts on Being Proud of your Price

One of the reasons people don't close a sale is that they are not confident about their price, which means that they wobble when the customers queries the price.

One of my main messages that I learnt from my business education training is Be Proud of Your Price.

In the beginning we obviously have to test our price. As well as working out the unit cost etcetera, we have to know if people will pay for our product. But if we believe in our product and have tested the market then we should be clear how much we are charging. It is up to us if we want to offer a range of products to suit different markets. For example I offer a sole trader's and not-for-profit rate and I also offer public workshops that are affordable for the smaller organisation and start-ups.

That is my choice. Whatever you decide is right for you. You just need to be clear why.

In reality, if you are confident about your price, people are usually fine with it.

However sometimes it will get challenged.

You can of course choose to drop your price if it will benefit you in other ways. For a longer contract with a guaranteed income I will offer a more mutually agreeable price because a substantial contract is absolutely worth it.

But, if you offer a fair price to everyone then be proud of it and do not worry about losing a sale to someone who doesn't want what you provide, because it is important that you attract the right people for you.

Goal Setting

Now that you know how much money you need and / or want to bring in, you can start setting the goals that will make that happen.

Most business owners, or not-for-profit founders, have not trained in business. We have an idea, a great product, or service that we want to share with the world, or our local community. We work hard to develop that and then, all too often, we are massively despondent when the crowds, armed with cheque books, don't come knocking our door down.

If we want to make something happen, we need plans and we need to write those plans down and share them. One of the main lessons I learnt in business is that we prioritise two things,

1. The things we enjoy doing.

2. The things we are required to do.

The systematic planning and preparation involved in bringing in clients is the thing that will be neglected if it is not written on our daily To Do list.

Goals give us a focus and direction and yet, **only 1% of business owners write down their goals**.

Plans change, of course, and with the rapid rate of change in technology and the global economy, the traditional 10-year plan is now neither feasible nor useful, but not having a plan makes it difficult to set time frames or monitor progress, which results in things just drifting. **Writing down a goal increases the likelihood of us achieving it by 50%.**

Sharing our goals with people further increases that because it makes us accountable and we attract and engage people who can help.

By having my written goals stuck on my office wall I see them daily. When I review them every few months, I am always pleasantly surprised by how I have hit my targets. Goal setting has two levels. Initially the **what I'd like to achieve during this period**, which I put as post-its or a time line on my wall, and then **written goals** which should be **SMART**, as in:

* Specific
* Measurable
* Achievable
* Realistic
* Time bound

And, of course, make sure at least one of them scares the pants off you!

An example of a **SMART** target in my business is

* Specific: To deliver paid workshops on ethical sales.
* Measurable: 3 workshops.
* Achievable: Yes if I make contact with the right people.
* Realistic: Yes within this time scale.
* Time bound: By June 2015

At the end of 2013, I set myself a goal of starting to write this book by Summer 2014. I wrote that down and I shared that with people. I started writing it as planned - and then got stuck, because I hadn't produced a **SMART** plan. Luckily, because I had shared this goal with people, I was not only accountable, but I got lots of help to get back on track - and here it is.

For those of us who are *solopreneurs*, life can feel tough, as we don't have a team with whom we can share ideas. I absolutely could not make the progress that I do without having supportive people around me. For that reason I totally recommend a coach or mentor, as well as surrounding ourselves with people who get us and our intentions and can hold us accountable.

> *Because all of us need a helping hand,*
> *and a kick up the bum sometimes.*

Task Nine

What do you want to achieve in your business over the next 6 months?

Having completed this section, you may have to hand some things over to someone else. We neither have to be, nor can be, good at everything, so outsourcing or employing people is a great plan. Trying to juggle too many things is exhausting and not conducive to growth. The most successful organisations have staff working to their individual strengths.

This is the end of the preparation part of the book. From here on it is all about the sales process.

*Before you move on to that, take some time to reflect on what you have read so far and write down 2 things you want to take action on. Don't forget to add a time scale and a review date.

The elevator to success is out of order, you'll have to take the stairs, one step at a time.

Joe Girard

Success
occurs when
Opportunity
meets preparation.

\- Zig Ziglar

Section 3: The Steps to Sales

We have completed section one, at this point you should have:

1. Done your preparation work;

2. Increased your understanding of your feelings about money;

3. Worked out how many customers you will need to thrive this year;

4. Thought about how you want your customers to feel.

The next Section, and the remainder of the book, will look at **why** people **don't** buy and then work through the key elements required for successful ethical selling.

Let's start with looking at the reasons Why people Don't buy..

Overall there are five main reasons:

* **They've never heard of you**. You may have the perfect solution for someone, but if they have never heard of you, they are not going to be your customer.

* **People don't relate to you**. You are out there marketing and networking but you are not using the language of your customers, so they just don't get what you can do for them.

* **This isn't the right time**. Most of us will buy something now that we wouldn't have bought 10 years ago, because our situations change. But we can't sell someone something they don't need yet. However, we can stay in touch with them.

* **They are never likely to be your customer**. There are people who are never likely to need what you are selling and that's OK. Our job is to find the ones that do need us.

* **They tried it and don't like it**. If your customers didn't like the experience they had with you they will not come back – unless you fix it.

Addressing these issues is the focus of the rest of the book and I have broken this into chapters that broadly cover making it easy for people to:

* Find you.

* Buy from you.

* Have a long and happy relationship with you.

One

Making it easy for your customers to find you

Build it and they will come may work occasionally, but mostly it's just not that easy. Unfortunately many new business owners have been sold the myth that if you set up an expensive website or get a load of flyers out, your customers will come rolling in.

Finding your customers is the hard bit, the bit that requires planning and focus and monitoring. It's a busy, noisy world out there and if people don't know about you, how are they meant to come knocking? As business owners, it's our job to ensure that it's as easy as possible for our customers to find us. So in this section we are going to look at the need to:

* Identify and understand our customers.

* Help our potential customers to find us **and** relate to us.

This is a substantial chapter because without these bits in place there won't be any sales.

FACT: The odds of someone randomly finding your website and buying is pretty darn low.

FACT: People need to see something three to five times before it's familiar - and we rarely buy something totally unknown to us.

In reality, the story for most business owners is; we have an idea, we may do some market research, we bust a gut to bring this idea to life and then we are massively underwhelmed by the number of people knocking on our door, or buying from our website.[25]

---

25 After a trip to the Edinburgh festival last year to see my lovely friend Annie Neat's performance, I wrote a post "Why working your ar*e off isn't enough..." http://www.janebinnion.com/working-just-aint-enough/

So why aren't your customers queuing round the block for you?

This is likely because you forgot to tell people?

There are people out there, **right now**, looking for exactly what you offer. If they can't find you, guess what they will do?

A man on one of my courses broke my heart when he told me that, as a start-up, he had been encouraged to spend £4000 getting leaflets produced and delivered – resulting in not one single enquiry.

Of course most business owners are not trained in marketing and without a plan, it's all too easy to spend a lot of money on mis-directed marketing. Start-up's paying for leaflets or newspaper adverts is common but usually it's the same disappointing outcome. This does not mean that those forms of advertising are wrong. The point is that one random leaflet through someone's door, or one advert in the local press, unless it's really timely, will rarely bring a return, because people need to see something 3 to 5 times before buying.

Jo Fairley from Green and Blacks, gave good advice at a lecture recently when she said:

Do not pay for any advertising until you are well known

That sounds like a bit of a catch 22 though doesn't it? So how can you get yourself known?

Few of us have a bottomless marketing budget and so we need to make wise choices when it comes to getting ourselves out there.

Social media is a gift for small organisations

There are some great free PR opportunities, such as getting press releases published, or getting on the radio, but to get a consistent presence, social media is an absolute gift for small businesses. When used well it is possibly the most cost-effective marketing available. Social media isn't a place for hard selling, but it is a great place to 'meet people', build relationships, let people know who you are and what you do. The more good relationships you build on there, the more people will spread the word for you. For example, I am now in the position where people come on my courses because they saw the information in a tweet, or a Facebook post, from one of their friends.

Building good relationships has always been the way forward for business growth and relationship marketing has never been easier, so if you are not already using social media then get yourself out there **now**. I'm not going to go into great detail about the **how to** of social media here, but you can find lots of great content on my website. You can download my free DIY guide[26] and I can work with you and your team if you would like me to.

If you are already using social media then that's great, let's just make sure you have a plan, because without a good marketing plan, pretty much nothing else happens.

---

26 http://www.janebinnion.com/product/social-media-beginners-guide

What's the plan?

I am, of course, a big fan of social media and I actually do love the supposedly random relationships that develop, though I prefer to think of them as serendipity. However, in the beginning, if you are going to see any results and not waste your time, you need to get a strategy together, otherwise you're just using the highly ineffective and time consuming 'spray and pray' approach.

These are the elements of a strategy:[27]

Who do you want to talk to?

Not sure? You need to write a list. This is the preparation bit of sales, the hard work that you put in to reap the rewards. There are no shortcuts to this bit.

This is what Guy Kawasaki bluntly calls "Finding who has your money in their pocket".[28]

When I talk to my clients about their list, I often get sent a spreadsheet of data - which they have bought! That is someone else's list. Get your own!

People get a bit overwhelmed by **The List**, so to keep it simple, I encourage you to just have ten names on your list. Those names are the people that you want to contact next. When you have made contact with one, add another name. Carry a note pad (or your phone) and when you get inspired with a new name, **add it** there and then before you forget, or lose your inspiration.

To get started, think of organisations that you would love to work with, then break that down and find the names of the right people in these companies. With larger organisations the company Twitter site

---

27 You can download my strategy planner here
http://www.janebinnion.com/product/social-media-strategy-planner/

28 Guy Kawasaki *The art of the start 2*

is rarely managed by the owner, so do your research. Their website and LinkedIn are good starting points.

Don't forget about what is called the **low hanging fruit**. Who is right under your nose? Who do you already know who might be looking for your product or service? There is nothing wrong with getting these easier sales. They can give you those essential testimonials and referrals.

Don't file your list away. Have it with you, or on your office wall (see goal setting). Make contacting these people part of your daily To Do list and don't forget to ask people who may be able to help you. I like the six degrees of separation theory; it's amazing who is connected to whom once you start asking.

This is the step that, once you get it right, all the rest of the sales process will start to fall into place, because when you know who your target audience is, you know who you want to talk to and where to find them.

If you chase two rabbits you won't catch either

Russian proverb

One of the things that blocks people from list building is lack of clarity as to who would want their product. When I ask people to whom do they want to sell, the most common answer is **everyone**. Even if that were true, even if your product or service is appropriate for absolutely everyone on the planet, we still have to narrow it down to a few at a time for marketing purposes. If we try to craft a message aimed at everyone then we are likely to put out a bland, beige message that actually attracts no one.

The 'everyone' target is often based on fear. We fear that if we concentrate on one group of people then we may miss a sale. That's just **the grass is always greener** thinking which isn't useful. So spending time working out whom your product is for and who your ideal customer is, is crucial.

Making contact

Now that you have decided who to talk to, you have to make contact and get yourself noticed. My strap line is **'it's all about relationships'** - because it is!

We know that, given the option, people want to buy from people they know, like and trust.

So the more you get yourself out there, building good relationships, the more likely you are to get sales and referrals. And, of course, the more you sit in your office procrastinating, or waiting for the phone to ring, the less likely you are to get anything.

How do you make contact?

Whether your customer is a business owner or a teenage boy, you have to go and hang out where they are. Creepy! Not really. The key is to find out where they spend time and be seen there, be that Facebook, Instagram, a networking group, or the local football club. This is why your list as well as researching your prospects is important. The more you know about your prospects, the easier it is to find them.

However you choose to advertise yourself, finding the right places is the key. If all your customers are in the same neighbourhood, then a regular advert in the parish newsletter, or even in the post office window, can work. If it's industry led, then an article in a trade magazine or a stand at a trade fair may be the way forward.

The more familiar you become in people's minds, the more you can experiment with other kinds of marketing tools.

A great example of targeted paid advertising is Innocent's approach for selling their drinks. They were distributing to small retailers to prove demand and then they paid for billboards directly outside the main supermarkets' head offices! Expensive yes, but well thought out - and successful.

Face to Face Networking. I know that networking has become a big business, but it doesn't have to be expensive. There's lots of free, or inexpensive, networking opportunities out there now, and most networking groups will allow you to attend two meetings as a visitor. It's really important to make sure you join the networking group that is right for you and don't get pressured into spending £500+ on a group that you can't get to, or has the wrong audience. Of course, if you join, make sure you show up and take part.

Some thoughts on building rapport...

There's a skill to networking and many people actually find networking events quite painful. Just being in the room is not enough: you've got to go up to people, chat and engage with total strangers. Pretty daunting eh?

And most of us get it wrong - a lot. In traditional sales they talk about 'building rapport' and you will know from cold callers that the training in this is pretty poor. It goes along the lines of *'say this, then this, ask this and you're in!'* (I can't help thinking of a bad sex guide!)

Shut up and listen!

Have you ever been stuck with someone at an event who talks at you? Me too. Does it make you want to spend more time with them/buy from them? It's never yet worked for me. Telling me how awesome you are just turns me off. People who simply talk too much dominate both the private and public sector! I've always thought we would be much more effective if we talked less and listened more.

You can make more friends in two months by becoming interested in other people than you can in two years by trying to get other people interested in you.

Dale Carnegie, How to Win Friends and Influence People

*W*hen
you talk,

you are only repeating
what you already know.

*B*ut

if you listen,
you may learn
something new

— Dali Lama

Networking should involve a lot of listening. We have a very short time to make an impression so asking good questions and **listening to the response with genuine interest**, is absolutely the best way to engage, on and off-line. I'm lucky that I really do like meeting and getting to know people: I love to hear their stories. But if you ask me a question just so that you tell me all about you, I will notice.

My one big tip here is to dump everything you have read on building rapport and have conversations with people as one human being to another.

By asking people what they do, what they are interested in and what their challenges are, you will not only find out if you are in the right place with the right people, but you will also discover that this is where the magic happens.

I learnt very early on that I couldn't **sell** social media to people that didn't understand the point of it. Social media was new and confusing and scary and people were being promised results that were just unrealistic. So I learned to ask questions about their business, what was good, and what were their struggles. By doing that I learnt what the issues were for people and where I needed to pitch my marketing. I learnt that people were nervous about looking stupid and being patronised by people who talked tech' at them.

And that is how I grew my business, by being the social media trainer that talked Human and understood that many business owners did not enjoy school!

What Do You Want to Tell Them?

Content is king and queen on social media

It's a noisy place out there and to cut through that noise and get your message heard, you need to understand what your audience wants. As you begin to build good relationships with your ideal customers you will find out the main questions they ask you and what interests them. Then you can share good quality, relevant content - be that blogs, vlogs, news articles, top tips, or videos of cute kittens - that will attract more people **just like them**.

The more you find out about your ideal customer, the more you can get great content to the places they hang out. Try joining LinkedIn and Facebook groups, or Google+ communities, to answer questions that your potential customers ask. Be seen as helpful and you will become the 'go to person' for your subject area. If people know that they can come to you rather than searching the Internet, they will, because we are all busy. It is, however, important that you are consistent in how regularly you share content.

Look for opportunities. Move out of your comfort zone to get seen and get heard. Throw your card in the hat for the sixty-second pitch, volunteer for the ten minute seminar slot at your networking event. Look for journalist requests on Twitter. I responded to one and had my story printed in a women's magazine. I got two new customers as a result. I produce guest blogs for people with a large audience and I write a weekly column for Lancaster Guardian, which is fantastic local advertising, but it is a time commitment.

We only have so many hours in a week; so again think well about the most strategic use of your time.

When is a good time to stop marketing?

Peaks and troughs are the bane of a business owner's life. Everything is going great, then it goes quiet again. I know we have all been hit hard by the recession, but for a large part, those peaks and troughs are not a coincidence.

We have a quiet spell so we work really hard to get ourselves out there, marketing, networking and building our customer base. Then we get a busy period and think **yeah finally we've made it**!... and then it all goes quiet again.

Why? **Because we didn't keep our eye on the ball.** We thought the basics were taking care of themselves. We stopped letting people know about us, about what we do and why, so our potential customers went elsewhere.

Things change, so having enough customers now does not mean we will have enough customers in twelve months time.

It's happened to me, it's happened to all of us at some point no doubt and hopefully we learnt good lessons as a result.

If ever you find yourself saying you are too busy to do marketing and networking, it's time to get a new plan together. If you review the outcomes of your marketing efforts, you will know which are the best channels to be using for maximum efficiency and which are the most useful networking events to attend. This may be a good time to bring in an extra pair of hands.[29]

Making contact with the right people, but getting no response?

This could be for 2 reasons

1. You haven't told them what you want them to do. There is no call to action (CTA).

2. They just don't get you. What actually is it that you do?

1. No call to Action

I know a number of people putting out amazingly helpful resources who are getting no sales or enquiries, because they simply don't ask people to do anything. If you are blogging, a guest speaker, writing an advertorial, or just sharing a Facebook post, make sure you are clear what you want the outcome to be.

What do you want people to do now that they have found you?

Do you want people to visit your website? Leave their email address in exchange for an eBook? Leave a comment? Sign up for something? **If you tell people what you would like them to do, they are much more likely to do it than if you don't tell them.**

---

29 Additional Resource: Too busy to tweet: http://bit.ly/JBbusytweeting

2. They don't get you

Have you ever looked at someone's social media bio, met someone at a networking event, seen a company profile on LinkedIn, looked at their website, or even heard someone's sixty second pitch and realised that you are absolutely no wiser as to what it is that they do?

They might be just who you're looking for, but if they haven't been able to communicate that to you, they have lost you.

We have a short time to let people know what we are about before they switch off and move on, so if we are making the effort to get found we then have to take the time to ensure that we are **really clear**.

How do we communicate to ensure that people fully understand what it is that we do, and more to the point, how we can help them? Because that's the crux of it, people need an answer to 'What can you do for me? How can you make my life easier? Save me money? Save me time? Fix that problem? Make me feel better?'

Last Christmas, I had a novelty card come through my door. It was in a nice gold envelope with a real stamp on it. They had even got my name right. Inside was a coaster with a sticker on the back saying "Let's have a brew in the new year". *Nice*.

I thought I must know them, but actually I have absolutely no idea who they are! Their coaster had some initials, but not even an individual's name. I could have spent time researching them and I did feel sorry for them, but it was Christmas and I was busy. Clearly a lot of time, thought and effort went into that lovely, but pointless, marketing campaign.

They wasted their time because they didn't take the time to look at it from the point of view of the receiver.

On LinkedIn I get an invite to connect, so I check out the profile and find that it's **Mr Jones, director of A to Z company**. I am no wiser about who he is, or what he does. So I move on.

63

I get a new Twitter follower, I go take a look at them, read their 'bio', but they're using trade jargon and I don't understand what they do. So I move on.

I look at a therapist's website, the owner has shared their numerous qualifications because they think that is important, but it means nothing to me - all I need to know is are they qualified and can they stop my back ache. So I move on.

It's a noisy place out there

By doing the earlier work and understanding our preferred audience, we can craft our bios and sixty-second pitches (which I hate by the way), so that we are heard. If I understand you, you still may not be the right person for me right now, but there is a good chance that your pitch will bring to mind the very person that does need you.

Being concise about what we do is one of the hardest things for most of us. So one of the simplest ways of dealing with this is to ask your favourite customers why they use you, and then start using that language.

Next ask people who don't understand your business to read your website and your bio's and get them to summarise what they have understood.

The clearer we are about what we offer and who it is for, the more we will attract enquiries from well matched potential customers.[30]

---

30 Additional Resource. Finding The Words Bringing a new product to market? How to gain the Know, Like, Trust element. http://bit.ly/JBproducttomarket

Two

Showing Yourself

We have been through a very long period of broken community, individuality and anonymity. We are now at a stage where people want authentic connection. Again, social media has been a catalyst.

I encourage people to come out from behind their one-dimensional logo to show who they are and what they stand for - and what they stand against, because given the opportunity, people prefer to trade with someone they know, like and trust. If you can let us know why you do what you do, then we have something to hang our hats on.

Telling Your Story

A story about an egg and a banana

What have these two things got in common?

Firstly, these two products are more expensive than their alternative.

Secondly, there has been a significant increase in sales of both during recent years despite the recession.

Why? Because people are familiar with their story.

If I show you a fair trade banana, you may not know the exact story of that individual banana, but you could tell me what it stood for. You know that buying that banana means that the farmers are being paid a living wage and that there is investment into their communities and schools. We are buying so much more than a banana.

The same with free range eggs. You only have to see the logo and you know that those chickens are living a much nicer life, pottering around outdoors, than their caged counterparts. The people behind the campaigns for these products have become so good at sharing the stories with us that we all know them and mostly are happy to pay the extra pennies, because we know the difference that makes.

Innocent found that their best ever TV advert was *The Chain of Good*,[31] which connected us as consumers to the producers and showed us the difference we make. That makes us feel good about our purchase and therefore good about ourselves.

What 's your story?

Most people find this really hard. We assume we are not very interesting and no one wants to hear it. On the contrary, we all love a story. It helps us to relate to each other and feel things - and remember that buying is an emotional experience. What will switch the audience off is the big 'me me me' pitch.

To be able to tell our story well, we need to believe in our product and ourselves. If you can't do that then no one else will either.

What is the story about you and your product that will engage your audience and help them relate to you?

---

31 http://youtu.be/LeXgxN24loc

When you are clear about what is important to you, you will become even clearer as to who it is you want to sell to. **And** to whom you **don't** want to sell. All this work makes it easier for the right clients to find you, whether via a web search, or by recommendation.

I now have a 90% rate of conversion from enquiry to sale, not because I have the gift of the gab, just because the right people are contacting me and I understand them well enough to know what questions to ask.[32]

By putting in the work about your message, you waste less time at the later stages. If this chapter has inspired you to do something new or more of something, make a note of it in the following table.

Task Ten	
Action Points	
Done by Date	
Review Date	

---

32 Additional Resource Mission Statements, PAH! I want a story!
http://www.janebinnion.com/mission-statements-pah-want-story/

Three

Making it Easy for People to Buy From You

When discussing social media for business use, people ask me if social media can increase sales. I explain that it can increase enquiries. What you do next will depend on whether or not they turn into sales. And that is the point. If you are doing all the previous bits well you should be getting an increase in enquiries. If they are not turning into sales then something is going wrong. Either your communications are misleading, or your sales process is letting you down.

In this section we will explore the most common obstacles that are put in the way of the actual transaction and what we can do to make the sales process as easy and as enjoyable as possible for our customers – and ourselves.

If you have got to this point in the relationship with someone then you have been doing things right, so well done you! You may have put a lot of time and effort in and this is the point where it pays off, so let's make sure we are not getting in our own way and putting our customers' money into someone else's bank account.

Making it easy for people to buy has a number of levels...

Firstly let's just double check that your enquirers are clear what you offer. The clearer your message is, the more decisions customers have already made, so the greater your conversion rate from enquiry to sales, as people already know what it is you can do for them.

If you are attracting the wrong customers, you are wasting their time and yours, so you need to review what you are communicating. (We discussed this earlier in Making it Easy for your Customers to Find You.)

The more confidence you have in your product, your price and your target market, the more you will attract the right enquiries.

If the people you attract are not turning into paying customers we must assume that there's a problem. Far too many companies have blocks in place that turn potential buyers right off. That is usually as a result of not viewing the sales process from the point of view of the consumer.

Here are some of the most common blocks that may be in place

* An unreasonable wait, on hold on the phone, or in a queue to pay, because you don't have the right staffing levels. If I am trying to hand over my hard earned money and I'm made to wait for ages, because there aren't enough staff on, the odds are good that I will give up and leave. Leaving me on hold paying a high call rate does not make me feel good about the company.

* The dreaded one... putting ridiculously hard to read Captcha (the image with distorted text) on your website. When I see those I assume you don't actually want me there – so I leave and I know that I'm not alone in that. There are much more customer friendly ways of blocking the spam robots.

* Not getting back to people because you forgot, or you never got the message. We have all had this: we try to buy something; we leave a message and... nothing. So we go somewhere else. With so many channels of communication now, we must remember to check them all. I get enquiries via all social media platforms. It can be difficult to keep on top of that, but if you have a social media account you are telling people that they can contact you that way.

* Lack of payment flexibility. I completely respect that some small traders only accept cash or cheques, but you just need to be clear about that in advance, otherwise you will lose the sale.

You will no doubt have your own examples too. Now take time to review your own systems and check there is nothing that will prevent your customers buying.

> *If all your systems are customer friendly, brilliant! Now let's look at how we can enable customers to trust us by making it an easy Yes.*

Offering Tasters

Tasters let people know that you are so confident in your product you can let them try it first. What tasters could you offer to let people try you out? Downloadable 'How to' guides from your website in exchange for an email address is a nice first buy in. If they like what you offer they will stay on the mailing list. I deliver free seminars to get in front of a new audience or free 30-minute 'health checks' and free webinars. When people have tried it and liked it they will come back for more and tell others.

When my daughter and I were in Italy we found an amazing sweet shop, you know, one of those where you buy a single chocolate and it's to die for. The owner immediately offered my girl a sample of what turned out to be the best chocolate she had ever tasted (and she *is* a connoisseur), guess where we went every time we wanted ice cream and for chocolates to take home.

Offering Packages

A copywriter I work with was trying to get back into the market after being overseas for a while. He needed to bring in some income quickly, but hadn't maintained a presence here while he was away, so was pretty much the new boy again. I discussed with him the idea of just getting a great offer out there immediately. His plan was a £500 package. It was a very good deal, but actually £500 is a big commitment to spend with someone new to you.

Making it an easy first *yes* means offering a package that's a no brainer, an offer that people don't have to think twice about. **Then** if they like what you do they are likely to invest more.

Easy payment terms

There is considerable evidence that easy payment terms, for more expensive goods, increase sales. I have made a decision, on more than one occasion, to buy a more expensive version of what I had gone looking for, because I was allowed to spread payments over two years with no interest. They got a better sale and I got great furniture that will last so much longer than the cheaper versions. That's a Win - Win and the payment terms were totally painless.

You don't have to be a big company to offer payment terms. I have bought a painting from a local artist and booked onto a meditation course because they let me spread my payments rather than having to find the money all in one go.

Introductory offers

Whilst introductory offers may be a good buy-in, if I'm a loyal customer I am not going to feel valued if you treat new customers better than me. There have been test cases on this issue here in the UK, where large organisations have done just that and it was ruled that they had to offer it to everyone. So don't forget to offer your existing customers a bargain too.

Thoughts on freebies

Not everyone will buy. There are people, like me, who will go round the supermarket eating the free samples, but not buying the product. Although of course if ever a sample really rocked my world, I would definitely buy. What about those people that want your services for free? This is a difficult issue for many, especially those of us who are selling our knowledge. I do get phone calls asking, "Can you just explain X to me". We all get caught out and we have to trust our judgement. Be clear about what you will give away, for example I will offer a free 30 minute Skype session, or occasionally a swap.

We can choose to do charity work; the point is, of course, to be clear about the outcome you want and your boundaries. I know that it would be very easy for me to do lots of free work in the community, but that doesn't pay the bills.

I like to think that every time someone takes advantage of my generosity, it helps me to develop greater clarity regarding who I do and do not want to work with.

If this chapter has inspired you to do something new or more of something, make a note of it in the table opposite.

Task Eleven	
Action Points	
Done by Date	
Review Date	

We are all busy. If you make it hard for me to buy from you I will go elsewhere.

Four

Closing the Sale

So you have people interested in what you sell. Fantastic! You have done all the hard work and now they want to buy from you. Interestingly it is this stage, closing the sale, that trips up so many people.

People get into a pickle here for a number of reasons, often due to fear of rejection, or a lack of confidence in their price. This is the stage where all those insecurities mentioned in section 1 can rise up if we haven't addressed them.

So in this chapter we will look at;

* What does it mean to 'close a sale'

* How we may be getting in our own way at this crucial stage

* Some useful tips on how to close a sale

* What to do when our price is challenged

What is closing?

Closing the sale simply means moving from enquiry to a done deal, where both parties know that a purchase has taken place, the customer knows when they will get their goods and you know when you will get your payment.

In traditional sales there are a number of 'closing techniques', many of which get sales a bad name, as they involve perceived manipulation, pressure, or sellers making promises that they can't keep. But I use and recommend one approach, the one generally known as *assumptive*. That simply means that if we get this far down the road, I assume the person I am talking to wants to buy from me,

74

and that if they have any more questions they will ask. If I have got that wrong it means I didn't ask the right questions earlier on.

Why close?

Well I can safely say that, as a customer, it is massively frustrating when people don't finish the deal and I am left unclear as to whether I have bought something or not. This happened with a telephone company recently. I thought I had renewed my contract, it turned out I hadn't. Four months later was still paying £40 a month too much. Apparently it was my fault for not checking! Guess how that left me feeling about them.

Common Closing Obstacles

* **Misunderstandings**. The most common closing problems come from not listening well enough, which results in misunderstanding what the customer wants. If we ask good questions, listen well and present our information clearly and honestly we should not have any misunderstandings at this stage. If we have, we just go back and clarify.

* **Go away and think about it!** Another common obstacle comes from not trusting that our customers are intelligent adults who can make informed choices. If you use phrases like " I'll let you think about it and I'll call you" to delay a transaction ask yourself;

† What is it exactly that you want them to think about?

† And what happens when you ring and they are not in?

Imagine getting to the supermarket till and the sales assistant says 'I want you to go away and think about it'.

I don't know about you but I'd feel pretty confused and just a little bit silly. It would make me think I had missed something important. I don't want my customers to feel like that. Do you?

* Thinking it's unethical to close a sale. I had a very odd experience last year that resulted in a blog post: Is Closing the Sale Ethical?[33]

Closing is not about bullying, or forcing, or tricking anyone if conducted within an environment of honesty and transparency. It is simply the process that enables a customer to leave with what they wanted, rather than leaving frustrated.

Our job is to use our skills and expertise to make buying simple and enjoyable.

> I went into a shop and bought a second hand drum kit at the start of the summer. It was a long-standing ambition of mine, but a spontaneous buy. Had the owner said, 'go away and think about it' I wouldn't have gone back because I would have gone all rational again. And I wouldn't now have my lovely drum kit. It wasn't a rational buy. Most purchases are not rational they are emotional. It was a crazy buy and I'm totally delighted by it. He assumed I was adult enough to know what I was doing. He made it easy for me by offering me same day delivery and we had a laugh. How much fun was that purchase!

So how do we close a sale?

First of all just take a minute to pop back and remind yourself what was a good buying experience for you. Think about how you want to be treated and therefore how you want to treat your customers.

Trust your customer to know what is best for them.

The wonder that is the Internet means that today's consumers have usually already done a good amount of research by the time they get to us.

If we have asked people the right questions and given them all the information they need, if we have been clear about what we offer

---

33 http://www.janebinnion.com/closing-sale-ethical/

and how much we charge, then, if they are still there that is a pretty good indication they are interested. At which point I ask them:

1. What else they need to know from me;

2. What date they would like to work with me.

If there is anything that they don't understand they will ask. If they don't like what I am offering they can say *no*. They will tell me if they need to go and check any further information with their team, and at that point we will set a date for a follow up conversation.

An ethical trader will give people all the information they need to make a decision and then sell them the right thing for them, so that they leave happy and excited. Not confused.

Some questions to practice that will help your confidence

I ask questions along the lines of **when** *would you like to work with me?*

Other questions might be **How** *would you like to pay?* Or **When** *would you like it delivered?*

Questions like this help people to notice the detail that they may not have thought about, which again makes it a better experience. If they get all the way home and realise, for example, they don't know when you are delivering, that will cause them and you more work and will reduce their enjoyment of the sale.

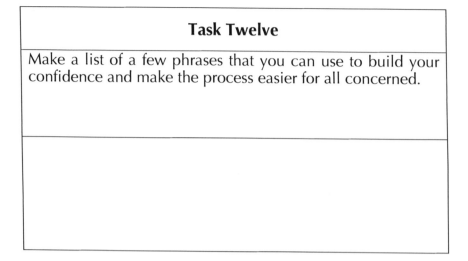

Task Twelve
Make a list of a few phrases that you can use to build your confidence and make the process easier for all concerned.

What to do when someone queries the price at this point

Take a moment and check the query, because they may just be clarifying what they get for their money, which, of course, is fine and you then have an opportunity to explain that again.

However, if they are saying that they don't want to pay that much, then what do we do?

* **Firstly, learn from this,** as it's likely that you forgot to ask some important questions earlier on. In which case you now need to ask more questions such as, "what is your budget?" and "what outcome do you want?"

* Recently I was asked about providing a service for £60 where my usual charge is £210. I explained that we were not comparing like with like, how I differ and why. Don't be tempted to sacrifice quality to match the cost: there are alternatives. If it feels like this customer wants to trade with you but they want to haggle first, find out what they can afford and offer accordingly. [34]

---

34 I managed to keep in touch via social media and they were satisfied that I wasn't attempting to force them to spend more but that I wouldn't devalue a quality of service, as it devalues them.

* If a customer's budget is below my price then I will explain what I can provide for that. For example:

† They could come on a public workshop rather than have in-house training. They can then decide which they prefer.

† You could suggest that you put them on your mailing list so they are kept informed of any offers that come up in the future.

* You can, of course, choose to drop your price if it will benefit you in other ways. For a longer contract with a guaranteed income, I will offer a more mutually agreeable price because a substantial contract is worth it.

However, do not fall into the trap of feeling that you have to drop your price. If you offer a fair price to everyone then be proud of it and do not worry about losing a sale to someone who doesn't want what you provide, because it is important that you attract the right people for you. (See being proud of your price.)

If this chapter has inspired you to do something new or more of something, make a note of it in the following table.

Task Thirteen	
Action Points	
Done by Date	
Review Date	

Five

When the Sale Doesn't go Through

In business, obviously, we won't always get the sale. That can be a tough one, especially if we have put a lot of work into it. Certainly, in the early days, it can knock our confidence and we may even take it personally.

In this section we will look at;

* Levels of success

* What it means when we don't get the sale

* How to look after our 'No not today thank you' contacts

* Addressing the common mistake of being in too much of a hurry.

One of the best things I was taught was **levels of success**.

Traditional sales are often seen as a game with winners and losers, but if you don't see it in terms of losing, then you can evaluate the experience and notice what went well.

When we meet with a prospect, we should have in mind what a good outcome would be. We may ideally like a sale, but there are other possible outcomes too. If you have followed **The Steps to Sales** you should know where you are in the relationship when you meet up. So if this is the first meeting, we could hope for a sale, but if that isn't where we are at then we need to decide what would be a good outcome.

Phil Jones lists these as:[35]

* Sale
* Prospect. This person is interested and may buy in the future
* New information. You know more about the company and what, if anything, you need to do next
* A referral. This person has recommended you to someone
* Make a good impression. At the very least we should have represented our organisation well.

They may not buy from you now, but if you make a good impression it is more likely that they will remember you and refer you to someone else, or keep you on file for future.

No, not today thank you

You may have built a good relationship with someone, but they don't want to buy from you. There are 2 possible reasons for this:

1. There are people that don't need you now. It's likely that most have us have bought something recently that we would never have bought 10 years ago, because it wasn't relevant to our lives or because we were not in a position financially to do that. But that changes.

2. Secondly your product isn't something they will ever buy. As a veggie I don't buy meat. That's fine, the butcher isn't upset, they don't need to tailor their products to me because there are plenty of meat eaters out there.

In either situation you won't get a sale from me. **However**, that doesn't mean that you can't talk to me, network with me, and be nice to me, because, of course, I know lots of people who do eat meat and if I rate your company, I will tell others about it. Never forget that we do not exist in a vacuum and everyone has networks of their own.

---

35 Tool box 2013

Also, things might change. Don't be in such a hurry! 86 % of people buy after the 5th to 12th contact

The slow cooker method

I have recently developed a taste for braised fennel. I have a bag of organic vegetables delivered and, twice a year, I get fennel. But I had no idea what to do with it. Then I found a recipe for braised fennel. This involves long slow cooking and it is gorgeous, melt in your mouth, delicious.

Slow Cooker

And that's just how some things are. Some things are ok for fast cooking and some things are better if you take your time.

I have *not today thank you* customers. They may never buy from me. However, because I stay in touch regularly via newsletters, networking or social media; because I share good information with them; when the time is right, they know, like and trust me enough for me to be their first choice.

This year I have had four people buy from me who have been on my mailing list for over three years. Simply, the time wasn't right for them then and it is now. If I had tried to persuade them to buy three years ago the odds are that either:

a. They were not ready for my training and they would have wasted their money and not felt good about me.

b. Or they would have felt pressured and just not engaged with me again.

If I don't need what you do now, but you stay in my life, if and when I do need you, you will be the person I will talk to.

Sales Statistics	
48%	Sales People never follow up with a prospect
25%	Sales People make a second contact and stop
12%	Sales People only make 3 contacts and stop
10%	Sales People make more than 3 contacts
2%	Sales made on first contact
3%	Sales made on the second contact
5%	Sales made on the third contact
10%	Sales made of the fourth contact
80%	Sales made on the fifth to twelfth contact

Source: National Sales Executive Association

These statistics teach us a good lesson. Making contact does not mean hassling people. It just means staying in touch, building relationships, paying attention and taking an interest.

We need to make it easy for our customers to stay informed. Letting people know what you are offering this month is painless, but might just be the good information that someone needs.

Social media and e-newsletters have made staying in touch very easy. If you're not using them yet, it's time to consider it.

Getting organised, adding people to my mailing list and staying in touch costs me nothing, but brings considerable rewards.

Getting Feedback

Some of us tender for work. It's my least favourite way of getting business as it's very time consuming, but I will do it if I see a significant benefit to working with them. If you tender and don't win the contract, remember to ask for feedback. It's good information for the next bid.

For example, I may have lost on price, in which case I can make some decisions accordingly. Equally it's good to know if I simply messed it up and I can I learn from that. We should not finish in a state where we do not know why someone did not buy.

If this chapter has inspired you to do something new or more of something, make a note of it in the following table.

Task Fourteen	
Action Points	
Done by Date	
Review Date	

Six

Developing great after-sales care

You have a new customer. Congratulations! Make sure you give yourself a big pat on the back and take time to evaluate what you did right, because this is how we build our confidence.

So that's the end right?

Absolutely not! That's just the start of the next stage - the start of a wonderful long-term relationship. A relationship where, if you look after them well enough, your customer may even become a part of your sales team.

In this chapter we will look at:

* The post sale stages that is Customer Care;

* The benefits of getting organized;

* The good economics of paying close attention to our customers.

This is a long chapter and for good reason. The post sale care is all too often neglected, but an ethical trader must pride themselves in how they treat their customers not least of all because this will make or break your company.

Customer Care

For far too many businesses, once the sale is complete, that is the end of the relationship in terms of putting in any effort. Any continuing demands are seen as inconvenient. *Which?* magazine did a study of energy companies and found that the phone is answered considerably quicker for new customers, i.e. by the sales team, than for existing customers with queries or complaints, i.e. *customer care*.[36]

Most of us will have experienced similar treatment; a classic one being with insurance companies that offer their best price to new customers and not to existing, loyal customers. We will quickly lose our loyal customers if we have no loyalty to them.

The message we get in these instances is "once we have taken the money we don't care". I talk to people about the **snog, marry, avoid** approach to sales. The examples above are **the snog approach**, where the relationship is very short term. We've got what we want and we're off!

Ethical companies will be seeking to have a mutually beneficial, long-term relationship with their customers, because selling a great product or service at a fair price is only part of the story when it comes to ethical sales. The marketing, sales and customer care should all be part of a joined-up strategy, because that is what the customer needs for a great customer experience. If we do not treat our customers as well as we possibly can, then not only are we being unethical but, with the speed of communication now, it won't be long before we are caught out.

Our job is to ensure that our customers walk away happy at the end of the transaction. Not neutral, but pleased with their purchase. And if they are not, then it is our job to fix that as quickly as possible. Because a happy customer will be a returning customer **and** a part of your sales team as they tell their friends and trusted contacts about you.

FACT: It costs six to seven times more to acquire a new customer than to retain an existing one (Bain and Company).

FACT: 86% of customers leave if they think the company doesn't care about them.

FACT: A dissatisfied customer tells between nine and fifteen people about their experience.

---

36 http://bit.ly/JBenergy

Which means that the minute we take our eye off customer care, we hand them to the competition.

Showing our customers that they are valued

Let's just take a moment to remember what happens to us if we don't have any customers. We can have the best product and the best team ever, but if we don't have any customers we don't actually have a business. There is a lot of competition out there and people do not have to choose us. Therefore, it's worth just letting our customers know how much we value them, isn't it?

I'm very clear that one of the best ways to lose a customer is to disappoint them. There is a bad habit of over-promising, that goes on with some sales teams that sets the organisation up to fail. I have met a number of former sales staff that left organisations because of this practice of prioritising sales targets over the customer.

So what if we turned that on its head?

We could under-promise and over-deliver! We are so used to poor service that anyone going the extra mile will get talked about as an exception - and that includes delivering what you say you will when you say you will.

What can you do to make your customer feel valued and important?

With so many cut backs we rarely get those nice little extras any more, so we really notice them.

What can you do that doesn't cost you very much but will make your customer feel good? A bouquet of flowers on the backseat of my new car really made my day, as does a thoughtful hand written thank you card.

Sometimes it goes wrong

We all make mistakes and sometimes our customers will have a less than 100% brilliant experience. Often that is due to expectation not matching up to reality, hence we should never over-promise. But we all make mistakes and mostly if we fix that as soon as we possibly can, we will:

* Be forgiven and

* Probably have gained a returning customer

I went to see a presentation by Jo Fairly of Green and Blacks, and the main thing that jumped out at me was her attitude to customer care.

> *The customer is never wrong, even when they are wrong!*
>
> Jo Fairly

Of course we *don't like to hear that our customers are unhappy*, but as humans, we all make mistakes. As tempting as it may be, it is never okay to try to wriggle out of those by blaming the customer. Treating those mistakes as an opportunity to go the extra mile and win a fan could just turn out to be our best marketing strategy!

Jo went on to say that she always uses a complaint as an opportunity to send out lots more chocolate. (Hmm now, what could I complain about?)

A complaint is an opportunity to build a better relationship with your customer. Most customers do not tell the company that they are unhappy - but they will tell others.

Some statistics to consider:

*For every customer complaint, there are 26 other unhappy customers who have remained silent – Lee Resource.

*96% of unhappy customers don't complain, however 91% of those will simply leave and never come back – Financial Training services.

88

Therefore, customer feedback is a gift and we should be grateful that they have bothered to tell us. So how do we ensure that our customers tell us when we get it wrong?

Let's think about dining experiences... In truth, as a vegetarian around 50% of my dining out experiences are disappointing. Of course, the waiting staff come round and ask, "Is everything alright?" and I say "Yes, fine thank you", because I know that their question is like the British 'How are you?'

I might want to say "Well this dish is actually a little bland and..."

But it is a closed question and I know that an honest answer is not what is expected. My feedback will cause a fuss and probably ruin the evening, so I eat up, pay up - and don't go back.

However, a question like, "Is there anything we could have done differently to make your experience with us better?" invites a different response, a response that makes the customer feel that their opinion is valued and brings us the feedback that we really need. If **we ask, we must be prepared to listen**.

Providing a joined-up service, because customer care should be central to all we do, not a department

I had an experience of investing in a pretty big domestic purchase about eighteen months ago. I made the purchase because I knew the company owner, he gave me all the information I needed and was flexible to suit my needs. Perfect.

However, he didn't do the fitting, he outsourced it, and the fitters were careless - after all, it wasn't their business. Resolving this and getting the property repairs done was a long, drawn out and frustrating experience. I obviously wanted to deal with the owner as I had bought from him, but I was passed on to the fitters who just had no investment in doing the work to a high standard.

As the subcontractors were meeting the costs, they kept taking short cuts and made a bigger and bigger mess. Because the owner made himself absent by this point, I was left disappointed and did not feel that I could refer the company to other people, despite the fact that

89

their product was good. The owner thought it was the fitters' responsibility, but they didn't care. **It is always the business owner's responsibility. Our company will fail or thrive by how we decide to allow our customers to be treated.**

I was obviously left feeling that once I had paid my money no one had an interest in ensuring that I was happy.

Interestingly over the last six months, as a customer, I have had to deal with the customer services departments of six national companies. Always the customer care staff were very nice, but they could do nothing about the carelessness and poor service except to throw money at the problem. These companies all decided that money was the way to deal with unhappy customers rather than tackling the real problems. To me that is fascinating, but uninspiring.

Some thoughts on growing your customer base

In traditional marketing training, you will be shown this funnel image.

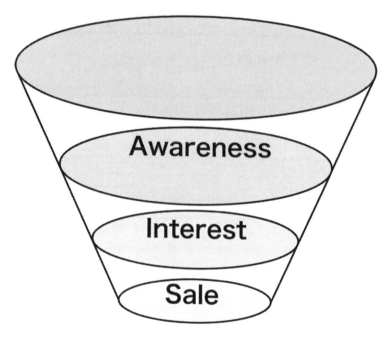

You market to a lot of people; some of those are interested and some of those buy. Essentially, shove a lot in the top and a small number comes out the bottom. I much prefer Ben Chestnut's reverse funnel.[37]

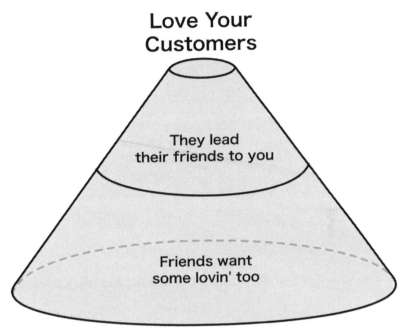

Love Your Customers

They lead their friends to you

Friends want some lovin' too

Some Try Out, Some Don't

This **grow your own customers** model works on the proven practice of: if you love your customers they tell their friends and their friends want to try you too. This word of mouth growth is particularly powerful with the rise of social media in our lives and is also referred to as *growing your tribe*. You deliver great stuff and the result is an organic increase in customers who like what you do and who recommend you to their friends.

One of the best reads on this concept is *Selling Happiness* by Tony Hsieh. This is the story of Zappos, the online shoe store, which became massively successful by having a philosophy of providing exceptional customer service. The model was that anyone could return anything and would be fully refunded. This took away all the

---

37 http://tinyletter.com/ben/letters/why-i-hate-funnels

risk for the customer and meant they were always happy. By using a loyalty business model and relationship marketing, the main sources of the company's rapid growth is repeat customers and word of mouth recommendations with over 75% of Zappos customers being repeat buyers. As a result, Zappos grew from a tiny company in 1999 to the largest online shoe company in the world and was bought by Amazon for $1.2 billion in 2009.

Thoughts on rewarding those who help you grow your business.

Of course what we all really want are sales that come via referrals from happy customers. People trust the word of their peers so much more than they do of any company advert. So rewarding customers who bring you referrals is a really good win-win option. I'm a natural connector and like to refer people to others that I trust, but I stopped making referrals to a company after I noticed that I didn't even get a thank you. I realised that was not the kind of organisation that I wanted to send my friends and customers to.

If someone helps you to grow your business how will you reward them?

A thank you with cake or chocolate works, as does a voucher, but you can also consider setting up a more formal scheme, such as affiliate links or a referral fee.

Another economic advantage of maintaining good relationships with your customers is that you can take a new approach to product development.

By listening to our customers, we can find products that our customers need rather than trying to find customers for our products.

Don't find customers for your products; find products for your customers.

- Seth Godin

Considering the statistic I shared at the start of this section, that it costs six to seven times more to acquire a new customer than to retain an existing one, this alone is an excellent reason to stay in touch with your customers. If my customers tell me that they want training in something that I hadn't been offering, I absolutely will look into offering that.

How much money are you throwing away because you're not organised? Or, what is a returning customer worth?

Forgetting to follow up with customers is a big problem that most small businesses admit to. But at what cost?

I was chatting to a business owner a little while ago, who proudly told me he never chases his customers and that they have to chase him. I wasn't really surprised that this man was not growing his business as well as he would have liked.

Most of us will have examples of times when companies didn't get back to us. I am reminded daily of one. About three years ago I bought some blinds for my office. I liked the product and the price, so while the owner was here I also got him to cost up for some blinds for my French windows. I'm good at budgeting and I explained that I would want them in about six months. Sadly he never followed up with me. I lost his card, he lost the sale and I still don't have any blinds on my French windows.

What systems do you have in place to ensure that follow up happens?

Do you have a database of your customers? There's lots of CRM (customer relationship management) software available. Some are all singing and dancing and pretty expensive, but many systems are simple and free.

We cannot possibly expect to hold everything in our heads, so it's worth thinking about how much you may have lost by not being organised and investing in a good system, or a very organised person.

If you have been inspired by anything in this section, to implement something new or do more of something you already do, then take a few minutes now to record your action points, set a done by date and a review date.

93

Task Fifteen

Action Points	
Done by Date	
Review Date	

Seven

The End?

So that is the end, or rather the start of the next cycle. Sales is a constant process of do, review, monitor, evaluate and adapt. It is about finding new and fun ways to build great relationships and to engage new and existing customers.

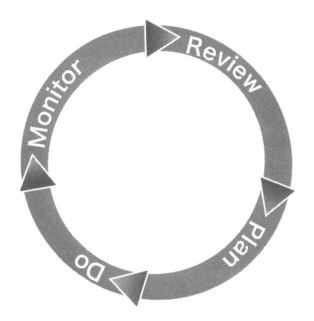

My friend Lisa Hooper who did my Q&A Sales Skills for Arty Types,[38] said afterwards *it's all pretty obvious really isn't it*. Indeed when we have learnt anything and joined the dots it mostly is all pretty obvious. But until we learn that it absolutely is not, mostly we just continue to act in ways that don't work. And of course even when we do know that it's all pretty obvious, that doesn't stop us sometimes taking our eye off the ball.

---

38 http://bit.ly/jbhooper

If things go skew-whiff for you from time to time come back and pick this up and check which stage you missed out.

If we are going to remain authentic, we have to bounce ideas around and share our successes and failures. That's harder for smaller organisations and so, as an added bonus, I have set up a Facebook group for everyone who has a copy of The Heart of Sales.[39] Please come and join us and let's keep the learning and the energy of ethical selling going.

If after reading this you would like some one to one coaching and support please just get in touch, I'd love to hear from you.

---

39 http://bit.ly/JBheart

Post Scriptum

Final thoughts

I said earlier in this book that writing this really bought my lizard brain to the fore, it brought up my wobbles and that resulted in the book taking longer than I anticipated.

What I learnt from this is

1. If we wait for everything to be perfect before we put ourselves out there it will never happen. Despite being read and proofed many times there will be mistakes in this book and people who find them.

2. By having a great team around me, of people who wanted to support me, I was able to identify where I was stuck and what had to happen next. We can't do that on our own.[40]

I have so many people to thank for helping me to make this book happen, people who have given their valuable time and hard earned money. So a heart felt thank you goes to:

* The people who believed in me enough to support via Kickstarter;

* Liz Neat and Frank Ledwith, for being critical readers. I am dyspraxic and without them I would have found it hard to structure it;

* Proofreaders Lucie Newmarch-Wright, Jane Scargill and Jonathan Bean;

* Carol Newmarch and Kristie Legg for listening and listening and listening and the Wobble Club just for being there;

* Isabella for not once complaining that I had papers in nearly every room for 6 months and that I burnt tea rather too often.

* Mark Keating for trusting me and spending many hours formatting and proofing whilst always maintaining a great humor. And the Shadowcat team who always make me so welcome and even provide coffee and donuts.

---

40 http://bit.ly/JBheart

Anyone who has never *made a mistake* *Has* never tried anything new
— Albert Einstein

Appendix 1

Q&A with Vix and Lou Lawson of Bough to Beauty

Tell us a bit about you and your business?

We are Vix & Lou Lawson, sisters who grew up in Lancaster. We set up Bough to Beauty, a company designing and selling quirky jewellery made from upcycled wood, in May 2014 and launched our online shop www.boughtobeauty.co.uk in August. We now have almost 20 stockists and also sell directly to our customers on stalls and online through our website and online shops. Our aim is to carefully select and approach our dream stockists in Lancashire and London, then grow the business from these two main 'hubs'. Our basic aim is to gain one new stockist a week and that is working well for us and we're now at the stage where we're getting repeat orders from existing stockists as well as 'winning' new stockists. This feels like quite an achievement for such a new company.

We lived in London and various other cities around the world for years before returning to our home town to set up our sustainable business. Vix graduated from Greenwich University with a B.A. Hons International Marketing in French in 2002 and went on to work in TV, advertising and marketing in London. Lou graduated from the University of Bradford in the 1994 with a BSc in Electronic Imaging and Media Communications, then moved to London to work in publishing, TV, PR and theatre.

We're passionate about sustainability and great design. We lived off grid and off the land in Portugal for several months whilst planning our business launch and try to incorporate as many of our passions into our business ethos as we can. We use upcycled wood to make our jewellery, recycled card and envelopes to package up orders and we've set up a local recycling scheme in Lancaster. We run our business in an environmentally conscious manner and encourage others to do the same, whilst making sustainable living fun.

When you pitch to people do you consider what you do as sales?

We're firm believers that business is all about people and relationships. If you have a good marketing mix, a clear message and people like your product, can see your products are good value for money and buy in to what you stand for, your products should almost sell themselves.

If you think of 'sales' as building relationships, it feels less daunting, most people want to work with nice people that they can trust and get along with, we know we do - for us selling is about making new friends and building new relationships.

How do you decide who you will pitch to?

We know our products well and having met lots of our customers on stalls, we know our customers pretty well too. It's really important to do your research and get to know your customers so that you can learn what they like about you. This feedback is invaluable and helps you to focus on what works and grow as a business.

We do our research before approaching new stockists, we make sure their company values are aligned to ours, which is important to us. We also give some thought as to which of our collections would best fit with their 'look and feel' and their brand. Each customer is different so this usually works well and shows them that you've made an effort and that they are an important customer.

We have a wide range of designs, including some, which are influenced by music, and more appealing to a younger customer and others that are nature focused and more appealing to older customers. It's generally clear to us, which of our design ranges would work best with different stockists and luckily they've agreed so far.

How do you make contact with the decision makers (and get past the gate keepers)?

For the most part we've been making contact with independent shops that we think our products would work well in. We have a wide range of designs so we're careful about what designs to take with us when we visit retailers.

We always look at the website at the style and the shop itself. From this we can usually work out who their target audience is, what demographic they will attract, and in turn which of our designs would 'best fit' their shop.

With our samples to hand we visit the shop. In most independent shops the owner/manager or the person responsible for stocking the shop, often works in the shop. If the person on the till isn't the 'buyer', once they see the products and realise that they would fit in well, they're usually quite open about giving the name of the buyer, telling us which days they work in the shop so we can call back and possibly a contact number, or email, so that we can take it from there.

We approach the person in the shop asking for advice on our products rather than being so direct as to ask if they would consider stocking us. We leave our wholesale price list and our contact details to make it easy for them to get in touch with us if they are interested in placing an order, so the ball is left in their court and they have all the information at their disposal to place an order or contact us for more information. If they have expressed an interest we can then follow it up at a later date when we have some news, e.g. new designs that we thought they might like.

A valuable tip we were given when starting out was, when calling up, don't leave a message, just try to find out when you're likely to catch the person you're calling for and say you'll call back. That way you're not going to annoy or harass someone, as when you get through to them it's the first time you've called.

How do you go about pitching to people?

We pitch to various people, using various methods, some more traditional than others. We have gained new stockists through Twitter, doing stalls at craft fairs, having pop up shops, walking into shops with our 'shop in a box' full of samples and attending networking events. What works is being friendly and enthusiastic about what you are doing and sparking up a conversation and seeing whether the people you are chatting to are interested in what you have to offer.

One thing I would say is don't get disheartened if someone doesn't order from you. In our experience the people who aren't necessarily going to be your customers can offer immense support in other ways. We've had people who we've just met put us in touch with their stockists, invite us along to networking events and training sessions; the support we've received is incredible.

We now feel that we're in a position to start helping other new businesses and are setting up an Ideas Club in Lancaster to connect local people, generate new ideas and expand our horizons. We've also been doing guest blogs with other small businesses we admire and who are working to a similar business model of ethical and environmentally conscious trading. We have featured them on our website, which helps both us and the guest blogger in terms of cross promotion on social media, raising the profile of each company in a gentle way to people who are likely to be interested. This is a nice way of getting our profile and name out there at the same time as other people; it feels far more natural and comfortable to us than a 'hard sell' approach.

How do you close the sale, as in take it from enquiry to done deal?

By asking. If you don't ask you don't get. If they like your products and want to order some, ask them if they would like to place an order. Give them the information they need, open the doors to negotiation. If they seem interested but are hesitating, ask if there's anything else they'd like to discuss or anything further you can do to help you to work together. They might want to know if you could negotiate on price or if you would consider sale or return. They might like the products but don't have room in the shop to display them or they've spent their budget for the month, or because they want to see how the products sell they might want a trial period. If you get to the bottom of why they are hesitating, you might be able to offer a solution that works for both of you; then they can place an order.

A good tip we were given was, make it easy for customers to buy from you and to find out more from you. There's nothing worse than wanting to buy something but it's really complicated and you're in a rush. You don't want your potential customers to give up on you simply because they find your order process difficult and time consuming

Personally I think the term 'pitching' is outdated and no longer relevant. If we were to come up with a new word what would you call it?

I'd be inclined to think of it as a sales chat, rather than a pitch. Pitch to me sounds like you're on the back foot trying to persuade someone that they want what you have to offer, when they don't. A chat sounds more like you're all going to a meeting on a level footing, to share information, find out about what you're both working towards and see whether you should be working together or whether you shouldn't.

It sounds more equal. You both have a direction that you are working in, and perhaps you both want to go in the same direction and perhaps you're not. Either way, it shouldn't be viewed as a negative thing. You most probably want to work with the people and businesses that share your vision and that you both want to support and help move forwards and grow.

We've often suggested meeting for a coffee, rather than putting a meeting in the diary. This gives us the opportunity to talk, show our samples in a relaxed, neutral environment and this has worked well for us so far. People like the opportunity to get out of their work environment, while it's still classed as work and most people like a nice coffee!

What are your biggest stumbling blocks?

I used to run market research programmes for several big name brands, (Selfridges, John Lewis, M&S, Virgin Atlantic), and I know how important brand positioning is, so pricing our jewellery has been a real challenge. Also getting our heads around wholesale prices and VAT has been tricky.

Lou was always involved in more operational type roles, so is used to being very organised but isn't very keen on the financial side, but then who is! We're both getting to grips with it now. It just takes discipline really, as it's not as complicated as you would think.

When we started we were terrified about the legalities of running a business: how do you register one, be sure that you're compliant, paying your taxes, National Insurance etc., but we got lots of help and advice. It's amazing how generous other people are, who have been through the same thing, so building relationships with other traders and small businesses has been invaluable for support and advice and we're really grateful.

Also we have a wide range of collections and they have a wide appeal from gift boutiques to galleries. We want our designs to be competitive and affordable, especially as we're only 6 months old and are still building our brand, but we don't want to undersell our work, so it can feel like a balancing act at times.

New technology can be a bit overwhelming to us as we're not the most 'tech savvy' people, but we've been on a number of courses and there's a lot of help out there to help you understand how to use all the fabulous new social media tools and apps that are available. We're climbing over these stumbling blocks and realising how useful social media is for raising our profile. Once we got over 'the fear' we've really enjoyed the immediacy of them and the wide reach you can have. We've had people ordering jewellery from overseas from using Twitter, which feels like quite an achievement, considering 6 months ago, we didn't really know what a tweet was!

Also we've taken the leap to and started using a CRM system so that we're not just keeping everything in our heads, which we were guilty of doing when we first started out!

Have you made any mistakes? If so what have you learnt from them?

When you're full of enthusiasm for a new business or project, the temptation is there to work with everyone that shows an interest in your brand. We went on a course a little while ago and were given some thought provoking advice, which was that, 'anyone who you work with is a weakness, as they don't care as much about your business as you do.'

Listening to this advice took us back to the organic farms that we volunteered on in Portugal. There were big groups of people working together as a team, often from different countries and cultures, with different expectations and values, therefore good communication was essential to get things done fairly.

The moral of the story: make sure you choose who you work with wisely and be clear about what you're all trying to achieve and what part you are all going to contribute. It sounds quite harsh advice to hear at first, but it makes sense and has proven to be true on many occasions.

Is there anything that you could put in place that would make life easier for you regarding your sales?

We now have Salesforce to manage our CRM data, but we need to get better at using it, especially as our business grows and more people are involved, it will become easier for information to get misplaced. Having these systems in place from the very beginning and getting into the habit of using them is really useful in terms of tracking valuable information, following up leads and generally keeping in touch with contacts. Make sure you look after your customers' data as it's one of your most valuable assets!

We're also so new that some things, like regular sales and cash flow reviews haven't been scheduled in as yet. These would help us to predict what turnover we need to be generating in order to grow at the rate that we hope to in the future.

There are only so many hours in the day and getting organised with the basics, such as sales and finance are so important, and will save time as it makes it clearer to determine what the focus needs to be on at any given time.

Without these measurements in place, it's difficult to see how business is doing and to plan a clear strategy and in turn to prioritise effectively.

What tips would you give to others?

Just get out there, meet people, talk to people, tell people what you're doing and find out what they're doing. You might find some common interests and be able to collaborate! When we'd only been back in the UK for a couple of weeks, we spoke to one of the directors from the local Chamber of Commerce and we were getting bogged down in the legalities and logistics of setting up a business and she said, 'Just do it; get out there, let people know you're here and start selling.' it was the most terrifying advice, but we took it on board and it was so valuable and totally the right thing to do. By doing this, you become aware of all the legalities and somehow these things do fall into place, usually by talking to people and asking advice.

So getting advice from entrepreneurs and business people who have experience, listening to the experts and learning from them has been a real shortcut in terms of getting the business up and running. There's so much free help out there, from courses on finance and business plans, to networking events, to mentoring and advice; the support we've received has been invaluable.

Last but certainly not least, be interested in something, whether it's music, travel, comedy, gardening, design - if you're passionate about what you do, whether it's work related or not, your enthusiasm will shine through, and we all like to surround ourselves with interesting and proactive people, don't we?

Appendix 2

A Q&A with Denise Armer and Jane Halpin of Lancashire charity Unique Kidz and Co

A bit about Unique Kidz

Unique Kidz and Co was founded in 2009 by two local mums, Denise Armer from Warton and Jane Halpin from Bolton le Sands.

Denise has two sons with learning disabilities and Jane has three children, her middle daughter has learning and physical disabilities.

Both had experienced severe difficulties, like many other parents with disabled children, when trying to find appropriate childcare in the local area to enable them to go to work. Denise had to give up her job in the NHS once her children had started school, because of the childcare restrictions she faced.

Jane's daughter suffers from Rett Syndrome and is also autistic and although she is 17, Jane still needs to find suitable childcare for her after school and in the holidays when Jane and her husband are at work.

So the problem for many disabled families is even more difficult because childcare needs to extend to these children in their teenage years and beyond.

With a clear demand for the provision of childcare services for disabled children in the North Lancashire and South Cumbria area, Denise and Jane refused to give up on their plans to return to work and instead decided that they would establish a childcare provision themselves.

Following over 18 months of grueling research, legalities, training and business planning, Denise and Jane established Unique Kidz and Co.

Neither had any previous experience in setting up or running a charity or in childcare but with the expertise of charity, childcare and special needs experts across the country, the support of other parents, and through their own sheer determination, they succeeded in July 2009.

Starting with just a handful of children, the number attending the charity's holiday and after school clubs has now grown to over 140, with children coming from across Lancashire and Cumbria to experience what the charity offers.

In February 2015 they moved into their own building.

When you pitch to people do you consider what you do as sales?

We don't really see ourselves as selling anything as there is no immediate transaction. We provide a service. We network with people and it can be 12 months later that they ask, for example, if we can be their charity of the year.

How do you decide who you will pitch to?

We have different audiences but we never miss an opportunity to network. When we go to an event we know what we want and we talk about Unique Kidz wherever we go because of people's connections and networks. That's how we recently got a patron.

How do you make contact with the decision makers (get past the gate keepers)?

We do go on a mission, for example we were determined that we would meet our new MP, but a lot of it is taking opportunity, such as meeting great people at the Inspiring Women Awards, we didn't know who we were going to be sitting with. Also we heard Phil Jones of Brother talk at an event at Lancaster University, then we saw him go and sit on a wall so we went and talked to him about our horrendous experiences of trying to buy a new printer and we asked him for advice. Soon after we took delivery of a new printer donated by Brother.

We don't always click of course. It's not always easy to talk to people you don't know, you have to be a people person. We are genuinely interested in other people and what they do. We always ask people what they do.

How do you go about pitching to people?

The charity is now 5 years old. For the first 2 years we never left Jane's bedroom we were just learning all we needed to learn about setting up after school play provision for children with disabilities. When we talk to people it's about the purpose and the difference it makes to our own lives, giving us our confidence back and a voice and we can answer questions.

We can now stand up and talk to 100 people when before we couldn't talk to 1 person without crying. The more that people listen and engage with us the more it builds our confidence that what we are saying is interesting to them. In terms of what we need we ask for money, time and expertise.

We have got to the point where we realise people can just say No, but we have also learnt that there are people who are just waiting to be asked. The more successful we are and the more we build a good reputation, the more people come to us to get involved.

How do you close the sale, as in take it from enquiry to done deal?

Businesses want to know their ROI, what's in it for them. We appreciate how hard businesses work for their money. We ask them what they are looking for and ask what we can do for them.

For example when giving donations for the ball, in the past we were advised to be prescriptive, but we have learned to be flexible and so **we ask businesses what they want.** That works better for all of us. We try to give back to people and keep it extremely people focused and we try to make sure smaller businesses can join in too.

We talk from the heart, we tell our story and we invite people to meet the staff and children to see exactly what it is we do for themselves and we plan to do more of that.

What are your biggest stumbling blocks?

There have been a few!

The biggest is our own family situations. There are many evening things that we just can't get to as we have our own unique children to look after, so going out in the evening is hard. So we need to have other people to attend things we can't go to. But businesses do appreciate what we have done. Then, Time, Knowledge and Skills. We have had to teach ourselves EVERYTHING.

But you need a mix of people and we had to learn to let go, to hand over to others that have the skills to do things better than we can - and to trust them. It was when we started to get a new office that we learnt that we are not office people, but *people* people. So we took on office staff.

Have you made any mistakes?
If so what have you learnt from them?

We have made mistakes because of inexperience.

Probably the main one was not following up. For example we have met so many celebrities it's untrue, but we don't have time and we are not good at collating the information for following all that up.

All we wanted was an after school club for our kids, we never knew all this would come with it. It can feel like an enormous responsibility on our shoulders. We have trustees who we go to for specific advice but we also buy in expertise, or businesses donate their specific skills to help us. For a charity it's not always about money.

Charities are businesses and need to run like that, but there is more red tape involved with a charity. Our biggest learning is how to keep the sanity within the family.

What tips would you give to others?

Never take your eye off the ball. Our purpose is to deliver a service and we can never take our eye off that.

Just put yourself forward and be yourself We talk from the heart because that is what we are about. We had never ever used power point until this year!

`When we had just started we went to a women in business event and we were pretty scared. But we learnt things. We now dress appropriately for the event and for our confidence to fit in and walk our talk.

We go by first impressions. Trust your instinct. If something sounds too good to be true it usually is.

We live by Sumo Guy Paul McGee's *S.U.M.O; Shut up , move on.* He asks "on a scale of 1 to 10 how bad is this". We have had an 8, but that's the worst it's been. It keeps things in perspective and makes you remember what matters.

We have never fallen out, we are a double act and we take on board each other's thoughts, and mistakes. We talk about it and laugh.

112

Look after your families and your staff team and last but not least, don't forget to take care of yourself. This is something we often forget and sometimes we stretch ourselves too much.

Is there anything that you could put in place that would make life easier for you regarding your sales?

We have someone that is just implementing systems to collate everything so we remember to follow up and not miss opportunities.

Appendix 3: About the Author

Jane Binnion is the director of JaneBinnion.com a social media and ethical sales training company. Jane regularly works with small to medium sized enterprises, micro-businesses and not-for-profit organisations.

Jane's background was as a youth and community worker in Birmingham, and later Lancashire. Jane studied and passed several business qualifications before moving from public sector to being an entrepreneur. Jane is the recipient of several business awards both local and regional.

Jane is dyspraxic and is a strong advocate of rights for people of all abilities. She is an avid traveller who delights in the restorative powers of long walks in the wilderness. Jane lives in Lancaster with her daughter and 3-legged dog. Jane is not new to writing, she writes a weekly column for the *Lancaster Guardian* and has authored other works.

Other titles by Jane are: *Super Women of Lancashire* - a collection of stories of twenty-six ordinary women who chose: entrepreneurship: http://bit.ly/JBentrepreneur; *You're so clumsy Charley* – the first children's book addressing dyspraxia: http://bit.ly/jbclumsycharley.

You can connect with Jane via:

Facebook https://www.facebook.com/ethicalsalestraining
Twitter https://twitter.com/janebinnion
LinkedIn https://uk.linkedin.com/in/janebinnion

Appendix 4: Sources

Maya Angelou Image: http://bit.ly/JBmayaangelou

Mae West Image: http://bit.ly/JBMaeWest

Will Smith Image: http://bit.ly/JBWillSmith

Zig Ziglar Image: http://bit.ly/JBZigZiglar

Dalai Lama Image: http://bit.ly/JBDalaiLama
"Dalailama1 20121014 4639" by *christopher* - Flickr:
dalailama1_20121014_4639. Licensed under CC BY 2.0 via
Wikimedia Commons.

Egg Image: http://www.morguefile.com/archive/display/187995

Banana Image: http://www.morguefile.com/archive/display/226072

Seth Godin Image: http://bit.ly/JBsethGodin
"Seth Godin in 2009" by Joi Ito - Seth Godin. Licensed under CC BY
2.0 via Wikimedia Commons.

Slow Cooker: http://www.morguefile.com/archive/display/832496

Einstein Image: http://bit.ly/JBEinstein
"Albert Einstein Head" by Photograph by Oren Jack Turner,
Princeton, N.J.Modified with Photoshop by PM_Poon and later by
Dantadd. - This image is available from the United States Library of
Congress's Prints and Photographs division under the digital ID
cph.3b46036.This tag does not indicate the copyright status of the
attached work. A normal copyright tag is still required. See
Commons:Licensing for more information.

Notes

Notes

Notes

Notes

Notes

Super Women of Lancashire

Celebrating the stories of ordinary women who chose
entrepreneurship [Kindle Edition]
Jane Binnion (Editor)
http://bit.ly/JBSuperWomen

As a single mum I decided to run a business from home thinking it would give me more time! The truth is I have never worked harder. I love self-employment, but I can't help thinking now and then 'oh for a wife'!!

So, after hearing so many familiar stories I decided to put together a series of blogs gathering up the words of local business women in Lancashire, sharing their successes and their particular

Super Women of Lancashire

Celebrating the stories of ordinary women who
chose entrepreneruship

Compiled by Jane Binnion
with
Foreword and Guest Entry by Rosie Garland

challenges. Celebrating our amazing super women; ordinary women being amazing, contributing to the local economy, creating employment and making stuff happen.

And that's how this started, a few guest blogs that just grew and grew. And now here are the stories of 25 women.

"This collection of stories about women in business provides a fascinating insight into what it takes for female business owners to start up and succeed in business.

I was struck by the diversity of challenges and tasks, both in their business and home life that these women have to deal with.

Jane should be congratulated for compiling such an excellent insight into the world of the Super Women of Lancashire."

You're so clumsy Charley

Jane Binnion (Author)
Colin Shelbourn (Illustrator)
http://bit.ly/JBCharley

Charley always seemed to get into trouble, though he didn't mean to. He was getting fed up of going to school, because he felt different than most of the other kids. Then he met his Aunty Bella... and everything changed.

This book is about dyspraxia, a neurological condition affecting 1 in 10 people, but it is still very misunderstood. We chose not to name it in the story because this book is for every child that is different.

"This book is inspiring. My girl is in KS2 at primary school and she opened up to me after she had read this book. We then read it together and she feels so much better to know she is not alone - and that someone has even written a book about what it is like to be her is awesome. My girl doesn't have dyspraxia, but she is made to feel different due to other things."

"I received this book as a gift and my son and I love it, it reminded us to enjoy being ourselves! A fab book that delivers a powerful inspirational message in a fun and enjoyable way. Highly recommended."

Printed in Poland
by Amazon Fulfillment
Poland Sp. z o.o., Wrocław

49690178R00072